DRAMA STUDY GUIDE

The Tragedy of Julius Caesar

BY WILLIAM SHAKESPEARE

HOLT, RINEHART AND WINSTON
Harcourt Brace & Company

Austin • New York • Orlando • Atlanta • San Francisco • Boston • Dallas • Toronto • London

Cover art: Joe Melomo, Design Director; Shoehorn, Inc., Designer; Andrew Yates,
Photographer; Mike Gobbi, Photo Researcher

HRW is a registered trademark licensed to Holt, Rinehart and Winston.

Printed in the United States of America

ISBN 0-03-057321-1

4 5 6 7 8   054   08 07 06

Contents

INTRODUCTION

Holt, Rinehart and Winston's *Drama Study Guides* offer you and your students a rich fund of information for understanding, interpreting, and appreciating a variety of plays commonly taught in the classroom. Teachers, whether they are intimately familiar with the play or have never before taught it—perhaps not even read it—will find the Study Guide an informative, creative, and time-saving resource. Students will find that the material in each Study Guide greatly enriches their experience of the play. The Study Guide will help them respond to the plays, aid their literal comprehension, deepen their interpretations of the plays, increase their ability to recognize and respond to literary elements, stimulate their creative responses to literature, and provide them with opportunities to exercise their critical thinking skills and their writing abilities.

Each *Drama Study Guide* is designed to allow you to teach the play in the way that seems best for your students and most comfortable for you. Many sections of the Study Guide can be duplicated and then distributed to your students, either as the entire class reads a play together or as individual students or small groups of students study a particular play on their own. The materials in the Study Guide are not intended to lead to one prescribed interpretation of the play but to act as a catalyst for discussions, analyses, interpretations, conclusions, and further research.

The following are descriptions of the major sections of this Study Guide.

Focusing on Background   Before they can fully appreciate any play, most students need some relevant background information. This section therefore supplies important information about the author's life, along with a brief discussion of his other works and philosophical orientation and comments on the play's historical context. For Shakespeare's plays the teacher is reminded of the rich background material already available in the *Elements of Literature* Pupil's and Annotated Teacher's Editions.

Critical Responses to the Play   These comments are excerpts of critical analyses written by Shakespearean scholars. They provide interpretations of aspects of the play. Students may use this commentary as a starting point for their own interpretive essays.

Elements of the Play   This section of the Study Guide first presents a brief outline of the play's key literary elements, which should be valuable to you as a summation of some of the elements at work in the play. It is followed by the play's cast of characters, a list that comprises summaries of the characters' roles in the plot and their relationships to one another. Next is a more detailed analysis of important elements of the play—such as theme, characterization, foreshadowing, and irony.

Some of the material in this section may be shared with students as they read the play; some will be valuable after they have read it. If students need a quick review of the definitions of literary elements, refer them to the Handbook of Literary Terms at the back of the *Elements of Literature* Pupil's Editions.

Teaching the Play   In this section are suggestions to help you set Objectives for the study of the play, introduce the drama to your class, and read the play with your entire class and with individual students. Here you will also find a section called Options for Teaching the Play, which will give you many, many practical and creative ideas for varying your instructional methods to suit the needs of particular students and particular classes.

Plot Synopsis   The complete plot synopsis is broken down by act and scene. It is particularly useful as a timesaver and is helpful if you are teaching the play for the first time. You will probably not wish to duplicate the plot synopses for your students because students might read them instead of the play itself. You may, however, choose to share this material with students for review, reteaching, or enrichment after they have read and fully discussed the play in class.

Guided Reading   Focusing on staging, characterization, plot development, and interpretation of action and dialogue, the questions in this section are designed to help you help students interpret the play *as they read it.* Questions correspond to specific lines in the play, and an answer or a suggested answer immediately follows each question. You may want to use these questions with students who are having difficulty with the play, giving them opportunities to follow plot and character development. Some students may find these questions useful springboards for research projects or writing assignments. If students perform parts of the play, some of these questions will help them think as directors or actors.

The following tools for instruction and assessment are provided for each act of the play or for selected acts. This material is presented in the form of worksheets, questions, and activities, all of which may be duplicated for students' use.

The exercises in the **Graphic Organizer for Active Reading** give students the opportunity to record responses and organize their ideas before and/or after they read each act of the play.

Making Meanings opens with literal recall questions (Reviewing the Text) and then moves on to questions calling for higher-level thinking skills, including responding to the text, inferential thinking, generalizing, predicting, extending the text, and even challenging the text. The Making Meanings questions for Act V require students to make informed judgments about the whole play by drawing on their skills of analysis, synthesis, and evaluation.

Making Meanings questions are designed for maximum flexibility. These questions, which are provided for each act of the play, may be distributed to students prior to their reading of an act so that they can read it with more focus. The questions may also be used for classroom discussion. Alternatively, they may be answered in writing as homework or as an in-class assignment.

Students should be encouraged to respond to at least some of the Making Meanings questions in writing even if you use these questions primarily as a basis for classroom discussion. Students may then record their answers in a journal or a reading log—a notebook of creative, critical, and emotional responses that they record as they read the text. Students may share, and use interactively, material from these notebooks with one another and/or with you.

Choices: Building Your Portfolio is a collection of critical and creative assignments for each act of the play that call for writing, research, performance, and artwork. Creative writing assignments extend the play to new territory. For example, an assignment may ask students to retell an important episode or rewrite the ending of the play in their own words. It may ask them to write an imagined sequel to the play or to cast appropriate contemporary actors in the roles of the play's main characters. All these assignments enable students to demonstrate creatively their understanding of the play. Critical writing assignments ask students to respond to the play through a critical-analytical route. For example, an assignment may ask students to respond to a critic's comments about the play, supporting or refuting those comments using

specific evidence from the play. It may ask them to compare and contrast two characters in the play or to demonstrate how a theme of the play is captured in a recurring symbol.

Choices activities also suggest research projects and assignments in drama, art, and music that take the student beyond the play itself and allow you to make valuable cross-curriculum connections.

Vocabulary Mini-Lessons, included for selected acts of the play, supply strategies for reading and understanding specialized Shakespearean vocabulary.

Words to Own Worksheets consist of exercises using words from the play.

A **Language Link Mini-Lesson,** included for one act of the play, focuses on aspects of style.

Language Link Worksheets, included for selected acts of the play, offer a hands-on approach to an understanding of specific elements of Shakespeare's style.

Literary Elements Worksheets, provided for each act, identify key literary elements in the play. Each worksheet gives students exercises to test their recognition and understanding of these elements.

Tests, reproducible for classroom use, are provided for each act. They include objective questions that are based on recall of key events in the plot, questions that require an analysis of literary elements, and short essay questions that cover the interpretation, evaluation, and analysis of the play.

There is also a **Test** for the play as a whole and one for **Testing the Genre.**

Staging the Play This hands-on workshop is full of practical suggestions that will help students present a scene from the play.

Cross-Curricular Activity This interdisciplinary, theme-based activity is appropriate for team teaching.

Read On This section is included for teachers and students who wish to extend their reading. It lists works by other writers that use topics or themes connected with the play.

Answer Key The Answer Key is complete, providing answers to objective questions as well as to interpretive questions, to which there is no one correct answer. In the latter case, several possible responses may be suggested.

Drama Study Guide: The Tragedy of Julius Caesar

Focusing on Background

The Life and Work of William Shakespeare (1564–1616)

by **C. F. Main**   C. F. Main was for many years a professor of English at Rutgers University in New Brunswick, New Jersey. He is the editor of *Poems: Wadsworth Handbook and Anthology* and has written reviews and articles on sixteenth-, seventeenth-, and eighteenth-century literature.

Every literate person has heard of William Shakespeare, the author of more than three dozen remarkable plays and more than 150 poems. Over the centuries these literary works have made such a deep impression on the human race that all sorts of fancies, legends, and theories have been invented about their author. There are even those who say that somebody other than Shakespeare wrote the works that bear his name, although these deluded people cannot agree on who, among a dozen candidates, this other author actually was. Such speculation is based on the wrong assumption that little is known about Shakespeare's life; in fact, Shakespeare's life is better documented than the life of any other dramatist of the time except perhaps Ben Jonson, a writer who seems almost modern in the way he publicized himself. Jonson was an honest, blunt, and outspoken man who knew Shakespeare well; for a time the two dramatists wrote for the same theatrical company, and Shakespeare even acted in Jonson's plays. Often ungenerous in his praise of other writers, Jonson published a poem asserting that Shakespeare was superior to all Greek, Roman, and other English dramatists and predicting that he would be "not of an age, but for all time." Jonson's judgment is now commonly accepted, and his prophecy has come true.

Shakespeare was born in Stratford-on-Avon, a historic and prosperous market town in Warwickshire, and was christened in the parish church there on April 26, 1564. His father was John Shakespeare, a merchant at one time active in the town government; his mother—born Mary Arden—came from a prominent family in the country. For seven years or so William attended the Stratford Grammar School, where he obtained an excellent education in Latin, the Bible, and English composition. (The students had to write out English translations of Latin works and then turn them back into Latin.) After leaving school, he may have been apprenticed to a butcher, but because he shows in his plays very detailed knowledge of many different crafts and trades, scholars have proposed a number of different occupations that he could have followed. At eighteen, Shakespeare married Anne Hathaway, the twenty-seven-year-old daughter of a farmer living near Stratford. They had three children, a daughter named Susanna and twins named Hamnet and Judith. We don't know how the young Shakespeare supported his family, but according to tradition he taught school for a few years. The two daughters grew up and married; the son died when he was eleven.

How did Shakespeare first become interested in the theater? Presumably by seeing plays. We know that traveling acting companies frequently visited Stratford, and we assume that he attended their performances and that he also went to the nearby city of Coventry, where a famous cycle of religious plays was put on every year. But to be a dramatist, one had to be in London, where the theater was flourishing in the 1580s. Just when Shakespeare left his family and moved to London (there is no evidence that his wife was ever in the city) is uncertain; scholars say that he arrived there in 1587 or 1588. It is certain that he was busy and successful in the London theater by 1592, when a fellow dramatist named Robert Greene attacked him in print and ridiculed a passage in his early play *Henry VI*. Greene, a down-and-out Cambridge graduate, warned other university men then writing plays to beware of this "upstart crow beautified with our feathers." Greene died of dissipation just as his ill-natured attack was being published, but a friend of his named Henry Chettle immediately apologized in print to Shakespeare and commended Shakespeare's acting and writing ability, and his personal honesty.

From 1592 on, there is ample documentation of Shakespeare's life and works. We know where he lived in London, at least approximately when his plays were produced and printed, and even how he spent his money. From 1594 to his retirement in about 1613, he was continuously a member of one company, which also included the great tragic actor Richard Burbage and the popular clown Will Kemp. Although actors and others connected with the theater had a very low status legally, in practice they enjoyed the patronage of noblemen and even royalty. It is a mistake to think of Shakespeare as an obscure actor who somehow wrote great plays; he was well-known even as a young man. He first became famous as the author of a best-seller, an erotic narrative poem called *Venus and Adonis* (1593). This poem, as well as a more serious one entitled *Lucrece* (1594), was dedicated to a rich and extravagant young nobleman, the earl of Southampton. The dedication of *Lucrece* suggests that Shakespeare and his patron were on very friendly terms.

Shakespeare's Early Plays

Among Shakespeare's earliest plays are the following, with the generally but not universally accepted dates of their first performance: *Richard III* (1592–1593), a "chronicle," or history, about a deformed usurper who became king of England; *The Comedy of Errors* (1592–1593), a rowdy farce of mistaken identity based on a Latin play; *Titus Andronicus* (1593–1594), a blood-and-thunder tragedy full of rant and atrocities; *The Taming of the Shrew* (1593–1594), *The Two Gentlemen of Verona* (1593–1595), and *Love's Labor's Lost* (1593–1594), three agreeable comedies; and *Romeo and Juliet* (1594–1595), a poetic tragedy of ill-fated lovers. The extraordinary thing about these plays is not so much their immense variety— each one is quite different from all the others—but the fact that they are all regularly revived and performed on stages all over the world today.

By 1596, Shakespeare was beginning to prosper. He had his father apply to the Heralds' College for a coat of arms that the family could display, signifying that they were "gentlefolks." On Shakespeare's family crest a falcon is shown, shaking a spear. To support this claim to gentility, Shakespeare bought New Place, a handsome house and grounds in Stratford, a place so commodious and elegant that the queen of England once stayed there after Shakespeare's daughter Susanna inherited it. Shakespeare also, in 1599, joined with a few other members of his company, now called the Lord Chamberlain's Men, to finance a new theater on the south side of the Thames—the famous Globe. The "honey-tongued Shakespeare," as he was called in a book about English literature published in 1598, was now earning money as a playwright, an actor, and a shareholder in a theater. By 1600, Shakespeare was regularly associating with members of the aristocracy, and six of his plays had been given command performances at the court of Queen Elizabeth.

During the last years of Elizabeth I's reign, Shakespeare completed his cycle of plays about England during the Wars of the Roses: *Richard II* (1595–1596), both parts of *Henry IV* (1597–1598), and *Henry V* (1599–1600). Also in this period he wrote the play most frequently studied in schools—*Julius Caesar* (1599–1600)—and the comedies that are most frequently performed today: *A Midsummer Night's Dream* (1595–1596), *The Merchant of Venice* (1596–1597), *Much Ado About Nothing* (1598–1599), and *As You Like It* and *Twelfth Night* (1599–1600). And finally at this time he wrote or rewrote *Hamlet* (1600–1601), the tragedy that, of all his tragedies, has provoked the most varied and controversial interpretations from critics, scholars, and actors.

Shakespeare indeed prospered under Queen Elizabeth; according to an old tradition, she asked him to write *The Merry Wives of Windsor* (1600–1601) because she wanted to see the merry, fat old knight Sir John Falstaff (of the *Henry* plays) in love.

He prospered even more under Elizabeth's successor, King James of Scotland. Fortunately for Shakespeare's company, as it turned out, James's royal entry into London in 1603 had to be postponed for several months because the plague was raging in the city. While waiting for the epidemic to subside, the royal court stayed in various palaces outside London. Shakespeare's company took advantage of this situation and, since the city theaters were closed, performed several plays for the court and the new king. Shakespeare's plays delighted James, for he loved literature and was starved for pleasure after the grim experience of ruling Scotland for many years. He immediately took the company under his patronage, renamed it the King's Men, gave its members patents to perform anywhere in the realm, provided them with special clothing for state occasions, increased their salaries, and appointed their chief members, including Shakespeare, to be grooms of the Royal Chamber. All this patronage brought such prosperity to Shakespeare that he was able to make some very profitable real estate investments in Stratford and London.

Shakespeare's "Tragic Period"

In the early years of the seventeenth century, while his financial affairs were flourishing and everything was apparently going very well for Shakespeare, he wrote his greatest tragedies: *Hamlet* (already mentioned), *Othello* (1604–1605), *King Lear* (1605–1606), *Macbeth* (1605–1606), and *Antony and Cleopatra* (1606–1607). Because these famous plays are so preoccupied with evil, violence, and death, some people feel that Shakespeare must have been very unhappy and depressed when he wrote them. Moreover, such people find even the comedies he wrote at this time more sour than sweet: *Troilus and Cressida* (1601–1603), *All's Well That*

Ends Well (1602–1603), and *Measure for Measure* (1604–1605). And so, instead of paying tribute to Shakespeare's powerful imagination, which is everywhere evident, these people invent a "tragic period" in Shakespeare's biography, and they search for personal crises in his private life. When they cannot find these agonies, they invent them. To be sure, in 1607 an actor named Edward Shakespeare, who may well have been William's younger brother, died in London. But by 1607 Shakespeare's alleged "tragic period" was almost over!

It is quite wrong to assume a one-to-one correspondence between writers' lives and their works, because writers must be allowed to imagine whatever they can. It is especially wrong in the case of a writer like Shakespeare, who did not write to express himself but to satisfy the patrons of the theater that he and his partners owned. Shakespeare must have repeatedly given the audience just what it wanted; otherwise, he could not have made so much money out of the theater. To insist that he had to experience and feel personally everything that he wrote about is absurd. He wrote about King Lear, who cursed his two monstrous daughters for treating him very badly; in contrast, what evidence there is suggests that he got along very well with his own two daughters. And so, instead of "tragic," we should think of the years 1600–1607 as glorious, because in them Shakespeare's productivity was at its peak. It seems very doubtful that a depressed person would write plays like these. In fact, they would make their creator feel exhilarated rather than sad.

The Last Years

In 1612, Shakespeare decided that, having made a considerable sum from his plays and theatrical enterprises, he would retire to his handsome house in Stratford, a place he had never forgotten, though he seems to have kept his life there rather separate from his life in London. His retirement was not complete, for the records show that after he returned to Stratford, he still took part in the management of the King's Men and their two theaters: the Globe, a polygonal building opened in 1599 and used for performances in good weather, and the Blackfriars, acquired in 1608 and used for indoor performances. Shakespeare's works in this period show no signs of diminished creativity, except that in some years he wrote one play instead of the customary two, and they continue to illustrate the great diversity of his genius. Among them are the tragedies *Timon of Athens* (1607–1608) and *Coriolanus* (1607–1608) and five plays that have been variously classified as comedies, romances, or tragicomedies; *Pericles* (1608–1609), *Cymbeline* (1609–1610), *The Winter's Tale* (1610–1611),

The Tempest (1611–1612), and *The Two Noble Kinsmen* (1612–1613). His last English history play, *Henry VIII* (1612–1613), contains a tribute to Queen Elizabeth—a somewhat tardy tribute, because, unlike most of the other poets of the day, Shakespeare did not praise her in print when she died in 1603. (Some scholars argue, on very little evidence, that he was an admirer of the earl of Essex, a former intimate of Elizabeth's whom she had beheaded for rebelliousness.) During the first performance of *Henry VIII,* in June of 1613, the firing of the cannon at the end of Act I set the Globe on fire (it had a thatched roof), and it burned to the ground. Only one casualty is recorded: A bottle of ale had to be poured on a man whose breeches were burning. Fortunately, the company had the Blackfriars in which to perform until the Globe could be rebuilt and reopened in 1614.

Shakespeare's last recorded visit to London, accompanied by his son-in-law Dr. John Hall, was in November 1614, though he may have gone down to the city afterward because he continued to own property there, including a building very near the Blackfriars Theater. Probably, though, he spent most of the last two years of his life at New Place, with his daughter Susanna Hall (and his granddaughter Elizabeth) living nearby. He died on April 23, 1616, and was buried under the floor of Stratford Church, with this epitaph warning posterity not to dig him up and transfer him to the graveyard outside the church—a common practice in those days when space was needed:

> Good friend, for Jesus' sake forbear
> To dig the bones enclosèd here!
> Blest be the man that spares these stones,
> And curst be he that moves my bones.

Shakespeare's Genius

What sort of man was Shakespeare? This is a very hard question to answer because he left no letters, diaries, or other private writings containing his personal views; instead, he left us plays, and in a good play the actors do not speak for the dramatist but for the characters they are impersonating. We cannot, then, say that Shakespeare approved of evil because he created murderers or advocated religion because he created clergymen; we cannot say that he believed in fatalism because he created fatalists or admired flattery because he created flatterers. All these would be naive, and contradictory, reactions to the plays. Shakespeare's characters represent such a vast range of human behavior and attitudes that they must be products of his careful observation and fertile imagination rather than extensions of himself. A critic named Desmond McCarthy once said that trying to identify Shakespeare the man in his plays is like looking at a very dim portrait under glass: The more you peer at it, the more you see only yourself.

One thing is certain: Shakespeare was a complete man of the theater who created works specifically for his own acting company and his own stage. He had, for instance, to provide good parts in every play for the principal performers in the company, including the comedians acting in tragedies. Since there were no actresses, he had to limit the number of female parts in his plays and create them in such a way that they could readily be taken by boys. For instance, although there are many fathers in the plays, there are very few mothers: While boys could be taught to flirt and play shy, acting maternally would be difficult for them. Several of Shakespeare's young women disguise themselves as young men early in Act I—an easy solution to the problem of boys playing girls' parts. Shakespeare also had to provide the words for songs because theatergoers expected singing in every play; furthermore, the songs had to be devised so that they would exhibit the talents of particular actors with good voices. Since many of the plays contain many characters, and since there were a limited number of actors in the company, Shakespeare had to arrange for doubling and even tripling of roles; that is, a single actor would have to perform more than one part. Since, of course, an actor could impersonate only one character at a time, Shakespeare had to plan his scenes carefully so that nobody would ever have to be onstage in two different roles at the same time. A careful study of the plays shows that Shakespeare handled all these technical problems of dramaturgy very masterfully.

Although the plays are primarily performance scripts, from earliest times the public has wanted to read them as well as see them staged. In every generation, people have felt that the plays contain so much wisdom, so much knowledge of human nature, so much remarkable poetry, that they need to be pondered in private as well as enjoyed in public. Most readers have agreed with what the poet John Dryden said about Shakespeare's "soul": The man who wrote the plays may be elusive, but he was obviously a great genius whose lofty imagination is matched by his sympathy for all kinds of human behavior. Reading the plays, then, is a rewarding experience in itself; it is also excellent preparation for seeing them performed onstage or on film.

Shakespeare's contemporaries were so eager to read his plays that enterprising publishers did everything possible, including stealing them, to make them available. Of course the company generally tried to keep the plays unpublished because they did not want them performed by rival companies. Even so, eighteen plays were published in small books, called quartos, before Shakespeare's partners collected them and published them after his death. This collection, known as the first folio because of its large size, was published in 1623. Surviving copies of this folio are regarded as valuable treasures today. But, of course, the general reader need not consult any of the original texts of Shakespeare because his works never go out of print; they are always available in many different languages and many different formats. The plays that exist in two different versions (one in a quarto and one in the folio) have provided scholars with endless matter for speculation about what Shakespeare actually intended the correct text to be. Indeed, every aspect of Shakespeare has been, and continues to be, thoroughly studied and written about, by literary and historical scholars, by theater and film people, by experts in many fields, and by amateurs of every stripe. No wonder that he is mistakenly regarded as a great mystery.

The Renaissance Theater

by **C. F. Main**

By the mid-sixteenth century, the art of drama in England was three centuries old, but the idea of housing it in a permanent building was new, and even after theaters had been built, plays were still regularly performed in improvised spaces when acting companies were touring the provinces or presenting their plays in the large houses of royalty and nobility.

In 1576, James Burbage, the father of Shakespeare's partner and fellow actor Richard Burbage, built the first public theater and called it, appropriately, the Theater. Shortly thereafter, a second playhouse, called the Curtain, was erected. Both of these were located in a northern suburb of London, where they would not affront the more staid and sober-minded residents of London proper. Then came the Rose, the Swan, the Fortune, the Globe, the Red Bull, and the Hope: an astonishing number of public theaters and far more than there were in any other capital city of Europe at that time.

Drama Study Guide: The Tragedy of Julius Caesar

The Globe

The Globe, of course, is the most famous of these because it was owned by the company that Shakespeare belonged to. It was built out of timbers salvaged from the Theater when the latter was demolished in 1599. These timbers were carted across London, rafted over the Thames, and reassembled on the Bankside near a beer garden—not the most elegant of London suburbs. Since many of Shakespeare's plays received their first performances in the Globe, curiosity and speculation about this famous building have been common for the last two hundred years or more. Unfortunately, the plans for the Globe have not survived, though there still exist old panoramic drawings of London in which its exterior is pictured, and there is still considerable information available about some other theaters, including a sketch of the Swan's stage and the building contract for the Fortune. But the most important sources of information are the plays themselves, with their stage directions and other clues to the structure of the theater.

The Structure of the Globe

At the present time most scholars accept as accurate the reconstruction of the Globe published by the contemporary British author C. Walter Hodges. The theater had three main parts: the building proper, the stage, and the tiring house (or backstage area), with a flag that flew from its peak whenever there was to be a performance that day.

The theater building proper was a wooden structure three stories high surrounding a spacious inner yard open to the sky. It was probably a sixteen-sided polygon. Any structure with that many sides would appear circular, so it is not surprising that Shakespeare referred to the Globe as "the wooden O" in his play *Henry V*. There were probably only two entrances to the building, one for the public and one for the theater company, but there may well have been another public door used as an exit, because when the Globe burned down in 1613, the crowd escaped the flames quickly and safely. General admission to the theater cost one penny; this entitled a spectator to be a groundling, which meant he or she could stand in the yard. Patrons paid a little more to mount up into the galleries, where there were seats and where there was a better view of the stage, along its two sides; people who wanted to be conspicuous rented them, and they must have been a great nuisance to the rest of the audience and the actors. A public theater could hold a surprisingly large number of spectators: three thousand, according to two different contemporary accounts. The spectators must have been squeezed together, and so it is no wonder that the authorities always closed the theaters during epidemics of plague. The stage jutted halfway out into the yard so that the actors were in much closer contact with the audience than they are in modern theaters, most of which have picture-frame stages with orchestra pit, proscenium arch, and front curtains. A picture-frame stage usually attempts to give the illusion of reality: Its painted scenery represents the walls of a room or an outdoor vista, and the actors pretend that nobody is watching them perform, at least until it is time to take a bow. To be sure, theater designs have been changing since World War II, and people have again learned to enjoy plays "in the round," without elaborate realistic settings. Modern audiences are learning to accept what Renaissance audiences took for granted: that the theater cannot show reality. Whatever happens on the stage is make-believe. Spectators at the Globe loved to see witches or devils emerge through the trapdoor in the stage, which everybody pretended led down to hell, though everybody knew that it did not, just as everybody knew that the ceiling over part of the stage was not really the heavens. This ceiling was painted with elaborate suns, moons, and stars, and it contained a trapdoor through which angels, gods, and spirits could be lowered on a wire and even flown over the other actors' heads. Such large sensational effects as these were plentiful in the Renaissance theater. At the opposite extreme, every tiny nuance of an individual actor's performance could affect the audience, which was also very close to the stage. The actors were highly trained, and they could sing, dance, declaim, wrestle, fence, clown, roar, weep, and whisper. Unfortunately, none of this liveliness can be conveyed by the printed page; we must imagine all the activity onstage as we read.

The third structural element in this theater was the tiring house, a tall building that contained machinery and dressing rooms and that provided a two-story back wall for the stage. Hodges's drawing shows that this wall contained a gallery above and a curtained space below. The gallery had multiple purposes, depending on what play was being performed. Spectators could sit there, musicians could perform there, or parts of the play could be acted there. Many plays have stage directions indicating that some actors should appear on a level above the other actors—on the balconies, towers, city walls, parapets, fortifications, hills, and the like. The curtained area below the gallery was used mainly for "discoveries" of things prepared in advance and temporarily kept hidden from the audience until the proper time for showing them. In Shakespeare's *Merchant of Venice,* for example, the curtain is drawn to reveal (or "discover") three small chests, in one of which is hidden the heroine's picture. Some modern accounts of Renaissance theaters refer to this curtained area as an inner stage, but apparently it was too small, too shallow, and too far out of the sight of some spectators to be used as a performance space. If a performer was "discovered" behind the curtains, as Marlowe's Dr. Faustus is discovered in his study with his books, he would quickly move out onto the stage to be better seen and heard. Thrones, banquets, beds, writing desks, and so on could be pushed through the curtains onto the stage, and as soon as a large property of this sort appeared, the audience would know at once that the action was taking place indoors. When the action shifted to the outdoors, the property could be pulled back behind the curtain.

Scenery

The people in the audience were quite prepared to use their imaginations. When they saw actors carrying lanterns, they knew it was night even though the sun was shining brightly overhead. Often, instead of seeing a scene, they heard it described, as when a character exclaims,

> But look, the morn in russet mantle clad,
> Walks o'er the dew of yon high eastward hill.
> —*Hamlet,*
> Act I, Scene 1

Shakespeare could not show a sunrise; instead of trying to, he wrote a speech inviting the audience to imagine one. When the stage had to become a forest, as in several of Shakespeare's comedies, there was no painted scenery trying (and usually failing) to look like real trees, bushes, flowers, and so on. Instead, a few bushes and small trees might be pushed onto the stage, and then the actors created the rest of the scenery by speaking poetry that evoked images in the spectators' minds. In *As You Like It,* Rosalind simply looks around her and announces "Well, this is the Forest of Arden."

The great advantage of this theater was its speed and flexibility. The stage could be anywhere, and the play did not have to be interrupted while the sets were shifted. By listening to what was being said, members of the audience learned all that they needed to know about where the action was taking place at any given moment; they did not need to consult a printed program.

Act and Scene Divisions

Most of the act and scene divisions in Renaissance drama have been added by later editors, who have tried to adapt plays written for the old platform stage

to the modern picture-frame stage. In this process, editors have badly damaged one play in particular, Shakespeare's *Antony and Cleopatra*. This play was published and republished for a hundred years after Shakespeare's death without any act and scene divisions at all. Then one editor cut it up into twenty-seven different scenes, and another into forty-four, thus better suiting the play to the picture-frame stage, or so they thought. But a stage manager would go mad trying to provide realistic scenery for this many different locales. Even a reader becomes confused and irritated trying to imagine all the different places where the characters are going according to the modern stage directions, which are of a kind that Shakespeare and his contemporaries never heard of. "Theirs was a drama of persons, not a drama of places," according to Gerald Bentley, one of our best theatrical historians.

Props and Effects

Some modern accounts have overemphasized the bareness of Renaissance theaters; actually they were ornate rather than bare. Their interiors were painted brightly, there were many decorations, and the space at the rear of the stage could be covered with colorful tapestries or hangings. Costumes were rich, elaborate, and expensive. The manager-producer Philip Henslowe, whose account books preserve much important information about the early theater, once paid twenty pounds, then an enormous sum, for a single cloak for one of his actors to wear in a play. Henslowe's lists of theatrical properties mention, among other things, chariots, fountains, dragons, beds, tents, thrones, booths, wayside crosses. The audience enjoyed the processions—religious, royal, military—that occur in many plays. These would enter the stage from one door, pass over the stage, and then exit by the other door. A few quick costume changes in the tiring house, as the actors passed through, could double and triple the number of people in a procession. Pageantry, sound effects, music both vocal and instrumental—all these elements helped give members of the audience their money's worth of theatrical experience.

Private Halls and Indoor Theaters

These, then, were the chief features of the public theaters that Renaissance dramatists had to keep in mind as they wrote their plays. In addition to these theaters, the acting companies also performed in two other kinds of spaces: in the great halls of castles and manor houses and in certain indoor theaters in London (which are called indoor theaters to distinguish them from theaters like the Globe, which were only partly roofed over).

Drama Study Guide: The Tragedy of Julius Caesar

8

HRW MATERIAL COPYRIGHTED UNDER NOTICE APPEARING EARLIER IN THIS WORK.

For performances in a great hall, a theater company must have had a portable booth stage, a building where the usual entertainment was a bear being attacked by dogs. The bear pits were vile places, but the temporary stages set up in them could easily accommodate any play written for the public theater except for scenes requiring the use of heavens overhanging the stage.

Something like this booth stage may also have been used in the private theaters like the Blackfriars, which Shakespeare's company, the King's Men, acquired in 1608. Although nothing is known about the physical features of the Blackfriars stage, we know that the building itself—a disused monastery—was entirely roofed over, unlike the Globe, where only part of the stage and part of the audience had the protection of a roof. One great advantage of Blackfriars was that the company could perform there in cold weather and, since artificial lighting always had to be used, at night. And so the King's Men could put on plays all during the year, with increased profits for the shareholders, among them Shakespeare.

Shakespeare's Plays

Henry VI, Part II (1590–1591)
Henry VI, Part III (1590–1591)
Henry VI, Part I (1591–1592)
The Comedy of Errors (1592–1593)
Richard III (1592–1593)
Titus Andronicus (1593–1594)
The Taming of the Shrew (1593–1594)
Love's Labor's Lost (1593–1594)
The Two Gentlemen of Verona (1593–1595)
Romeo and Juliet (1594–1595)
Richard II (1595–1596)
A Midsummer Night's Dream (1595–1596)
King John (1596–1597)
The Merchant of Venice (1596–1597)
Henry IV, Part I (1597)
Henry IV, Part II (1597–1598)
Much Ado About Nothing (1598–1599)
Henry V (1599–1600)
Julius Caesar (1599–1600)

As You Like It (1599–1600)
Twelfth Night (1599–1600)
Hamlet (1600–1601)
The Merry Wives of Windsor (1600–1601)
Troilus and Cressida (1601–1603)
All's Well That Ends Well (1602–1603)
Othello (1604–1605)
Measure for Measure (1604–1605)
King Lear (1605–1606)
Macbeth (1605–1606)
Antony and Cleopatra (1606–1607)
Timon of Athens (1607–1608)
Coriolanus (1607–1608)
Pericles (1608–1609)
Cymbeline (1609–1610)
The Winter's Tale (1610–1611)
The Tempest (1611–1612)
The Two Noble Kinsmen (1612–1613)
Henry VIII (1612–1613)

Sources for *The Tragedy of Julius Caesar*
from an Introduction to *The Tragedy of Julius Caesar*

by **G. B. Harrison**

The story of Julius Caesar had often been retold in story, poem, and play before Shakespeare's time, but the direct sources of the play were the lives of Julius Caesar, Marcus Brutus, and Marcus Antonius in Sir Thomas North's translation of *The Lives of the Noble Grecians and Romans by That Eminent Historiographer and Philosopher, Plutarch of Chaeronea.*

Plutarch was a Greek born in A.D. 46. He was educated at Athens and became what would now be called a professor of philosophy. He lectured at Rome and left a large collection of essays and learned articles called the *Morals*—once much read—as well as the famous *Lives.* These were a series of parallel biographies of eminent Greeks and Romans. Plutarch wrote forty-eight of these parallels, adding to most of them a brief comparison.

The *Lives* are not formal biographies giving dates, places, and facts but, rather, biographical and psychological studies of great men. Plutarch assumed that his readers were already familiar with the facts, and his intention was to portray character. He consulted the best authorities and preferably those who could provide anecdotes and sayings, for, as he wrote, "The noblest deeds do not always show men's virtues and vices, but oftentimes a light occasion, a word, or some sport makes men's natural dispositions and manners appear more plain than the famous battles wherein are slain ten thousand men or the great armies or cities won by siege or assault."

The *Lives* reached English readers in the translation made by Sir Thomas North and printed in 1579. North, however, went not to the Greek but to a French translation made from the Latin by Jacques Amyot and published in 1559 and 1565. A second edition of North's translation was printed in 1595 by Richard Field, who was also the printer of Shakespeare's *Venus and Adonis* and *The Rape of Lucrece*. "North's Plutarch" is a great book, a fine specimen of vigorous Elizabethan prose, for North himself was a man of very varied experi-

ence, with a lively mind and a superb mastery of words. There is no richer collection of historical material for a dramatist.

Nevertheless, to make a coherent play, Shakespeare had to simplify vastly the history of events between Caesar's return to Rome in September 45 B.C. and the Second Battle of Philippi, two years later. Moreover, he did not choose to follow the common pattern of historical-biographical plays, which usually ended with the death of the hero in Act V. Instead, he set the murder of Caesar in the third act and in the last two acts showed how the murderers came to destruction. For this Plutarch was partly responsible, for *Julius Caesar* is based rather on his "Life of Brutus" than on that of Caesar.

From "Introduction" by G. B. Harrison (retitled "Sources for *The Tragedy of Julius Caesar*") to *The Tragedy of Julius Caesar* from *Shakespeare: The Complete Works,* edited by G. B. Harrison. Copyright © 1968 by *Harcourt Brace & Company.* Reprinted by permission of the publisher.

Critical Responses to
The Tragedy of Julius Caesar

"Omens and Portents, Augury and Dream"
from Dreams and Interpretations: Julius Caesar

by **Marjorie Garber**

In the final act of *Julius Caesar,* Cassius, fearful of defeat at Philippi, dispatches Titinius to discover whether the surrounding troops are friends or enemies. He posts another soldier to observe, and when the soldier sees Titinius encircled by horsemen and reports that he is taken, Cassius runs on his sword and dies. Shortly afterward, Titinius reenters the scene bearing a "wreath of victory" from Brutus. When he sees the dead body, he at once understands Cassius's tragic mistake. "Alas, thou hast misconstrued everything!" (Act V, Scene 3, line 84), he cries out, and he too runs on Cassius's sword.

That one cry, "Thou hast misconstrued everything!" might well serve as an epigraph for the whole of *Julius Caesar.* The play is full of omens and portents, augury and dream, and almost without exception these omens are misinterpreted. Calphurnia's dream, the dream of Cinna the poet, the advice of the augurers, all suggest one course of action and produce its opposite. The compelling dream imagery of the play, which should, had it been rightly interpreted, have persuaded Caesar to avoid the Capitol and Cinna not to go forth, is deflected by the characters of men, making tragedy inevitable. For *Julius Caesar* is not only a political play but also a play of character. Its imagery of dream and sign, an imagery so powerful that it enters the plot on the level of action, is a means of examining character and consciousness. . . .

It becomes evident that signs and dreams are morally neutral elements, incapable of effect without interpretation. By structuring his play around them, Shakespeare invites us to scrutinize the men who read the signs—to witness the tragedy of misconstruction. The two senses of Cicero's maxim, the willful deceiver and the willingly deceived, are the controllers of dream and the controlled. Decius Brutus, perhaps the coldest in a play replete with cold men, states the position of the former unequivocally. No matter how superstitious Caesar has lately become, he, Decius Brutus, is confident of his ability to manipulate him.

> I can o'ersway him; for he loves to hear
> That unicorns may be betrayed with trees,

And bears with glasses, elephants with holes,
Lions with toils, and men with flatterers;
But when I tell him he hates flatterers,
He says he does, being then most flatterèd.
Let me work;
For I can give his humor the true bent,
And I will bring him to the Capitol.
> —Act II, Scene 1, lines 203–211

Willful misconstruction is his purpose and his art. And, fulfilling his promise, it is Decius Brutus who artfully misinterprets Calphurnia's dream and coaxes Caesar to the scene of his death.

Calphurnia's dream is one of the play's cruxes. By this time in the course of the drama, an internal convention has been established regarding dreams and omens: Whatever their source, they are true, and it is dangerous to disregard them. Shakespeare's audience would certainly have been familiar with the story of Julius Caesar, and such a collection of portents and premonitions would have seemed to them, as it does to us, to be infallibly leading to the moment of murder. Calphurnia herself adds to the catalog of unnatural events:

> A lioness hath whelpèd in the streets,
> And graves have yawned, and yielded up their
>   dead;
> Fierce fiery warriors fought upon the clouds
> In ranks and squadrons and right form of war,
> Which drizzled blood upon the Capitol;
> The noise of battle hurtled in the air,
> Horses did neigh and dying men did groan,
> And ghosts did shriek and squeal about the
>   streets.
> —Act II, Scene 2, lines 17–24

This is in fact an apocalypse of sorts, the last judgment of Rome. Unlike the events narrated by Casca, those reported by Calphurnia are not specified in Plutarch; it is noteworthy how much more *Shakespearean* they are and how economically chosen to foreshadow, metaphorically, the later events of the play. The lioness is Wrath, and from her loins will spring forth "ranks and squadrons and right form of war" while the ghost of Caesar appears solemnly in the streets. Shakespeare was to remember this moment soon again, upon the appearance of the most majestic of all his ghosts.

> In the most high and palmy state of Rome,
> A little ere the mightiest Julius fell,
> The graves stood tenantless, and the sheeted dead
> Did squeak and gibber in the Roman streets. . . .
> —*Hamlet,* Act I, Scene 1, lines 113–116

Calphurnia's bona fides as a prophetess is thus firmly established by the time we hear her dream, and so too is the blind obstinacy of Caesar. He willfully misinterprets a message from his augurers, who advise him to stay away from the Capitol, alarmed by the sacrifice of a beast in which they found no heart. "Caesar should be a beast without a heart," he declares, "If he should stay at home today for fear" (Act II, Scene 2, lines 42–43), thus completely reversing the message of the haruspices. In this mood he is interrupted by Decius Brutus, whose wiliness outlasts his own more heedless cunning. Caesar is one of those elder statesmen who visibly enjoy causing discomfort to their underlings; it is partially for this reason that he now abruptly changes his mind upon the entrance of Decius and declares, "I will not come" (Act II, Scene 2, line 71). We have not yet heard the dream; Shakespeare leaves it for Caesar himself to recount, as he does now to Decius.

> She dreamt tonight she saw my statue,
> Which, like a fountain with an hundred spouts,
> Did run pure blood, and many lusty Romans
> Came smiling and did bathe their hands in it.
> And these does she apply for warnings and portents
> And evils imminent, and on her knee
> Hath begged that I will stay at home today.
> —Act II, Scene 2, lines 76–82

We may notice that here, as in our interpretation of Romeo's last dream, the dead man becomes a statue; this is a recurrent conceit in Shakespearean dreams, and in *The Winter's Tale* the dream action becomes plot as Hermione "dies," becomes a "statue," and is reborn. In Calphurnia's dream the latent dream thoughts are not far removed from the manifest content. She interprets the statue as the body of Caesar and also his funerary monument, and the gushing forth of blood she reads as death. As a prophetic dream this is both an accurate and a curiously lyrical one, graceful in its imagery. It forecasts directly the assassination before the Capitol.

Decius, however, is prepared for the event, and he begins immediately to discredit Calphurnia's prediction. He commences with what is by now a familiar note, "This dream is all amiss interpreted," and offers instead his own "interpretation":

> It was a vision fair and fortunate:
> Your statue spouting blood in many pipes,
> In which so many smiling Romans bathed,
> Signifies that from you great Rome shall suck
> Reviving blood, and that great men shall press
> For tinctures, stains, relics, and cognizance.
> This by Calphurnia's dream is signified.
> —Act II, Scene 2, lines 84–90

It is the dissimulator now who cries, "Thou hast misconstrued everything!" He takes the manifest content of Calphurnia's dream and attributes it to a clever if wholly fabricated set of latent thoughts, which are the more impressive for their psychological insight. Caesar is flattered, as Decius had predicted, and resolves to go to the Capitol. His last doubts are abruptly erased when Decius suggests that he will be offered a crown and warns that refusal to go will seem like uxoriousness:

> . . . It were a mock
> Apt to be rendered, for someone to say
> "Break up the Senate till another time,
> When Caesar's wife shall meet with better dreams."
> —Act II, Scene 2, lines 96–99

This is a thrust well calculated to strike home. But there is a curious ambiguity about Calphurnia's dream, and the real irony of the situation is that Decius' spurious interpretation of it is as true in its way as Calphurnia's. . . .

Julius Caesar is a complex and ambiguous play that does not concern itself principally with political theory but, rather, with the strange blindness of the rational mind—in politics and elsewhere—to the great irrational powers that flow through life and control it. The significance attached to the theme of "thou hast misconstrued everything" clearly depends to a large extent upon the reading—or misreading—of the play's many dreams. Here, in the last of his plays to use dreams and omens primarily as devices of plot, Shakespeare again demonstrates the great symbolic power that resides in the dream, together with its remarkable capacity for elucidating aspects of the play which otherwise remain in shadow.

From "Dreams and Interpretations: *Julius Caesar*" (retitled "Omens and Portents, Augury and Dream") from *Dream in Shakespeare: From Metaphor to Metamorphosis* by Marjorie B. Garber. Copyright © 1974 by *Yale University Press*. Reprinted by permission of the publisher.

"A Tragic Chronicle"
from *Julius Caesar and Plutarch*
by Geoffrey Bullough

In action, *Julius Caesar* is a tragic chronicle with three main focuses: the seduction of Brutus; the assassination and its concomitants; and the vengeance of Antony, in which his rise and Octavius's are contrasted with the decline and fall of Brutus and Cassius. The foregoing analysis shows that Shakespeare drew freely throughout on Plutarch's three *Lives*. Probably the fact that he had three biographies before him suggested a threefold division, in which first Brutus was the main (though not the only) center of interest, then Caesar, and lastly Antony with Octavius. Having to piece together the deeds and motives of the participants out of three accounts, Shakespeare was encouraged not to make any of them—the noble conspirator, the world-famous victim, the dexterous avenger—into the sole hero of his play. His own interest seems to have been divided among them, and since in Plutarch and other histories none of the three was above reproach, and all were portrayed with a mixture of approval and disapproval, the paradoxes of motivation and morality seem to have seized Shakespeare's imagination and inspired or fortified his disinclination to make any one of them the central figure. Rather, he prefers to give a balanced view, pointing out the mingled good and evil in their behavior, without explicit moralizing. . . . His studies in English history had shown him how mixed was human nature both in politics and in private life; and the comedies he was perhaps already writing or planning . . . were to be darker in tone than his previous ones, because in them romance was to be treated realistically in the light of deep ethical conflict.

So Julius Caesar is not the "hero," although he is the pivot of the tragedy. He is the world victor, as even Cassius bitterly admits:

Why, man, he doth bestride the narrow world
Like a Colossus. . . .
—Act I, Scene 2, lines 133–136

He has "the start of the majestic world," to "bear the palm alone." He has conquered the Pompeys, and Shakespeare could depend on his audience to have the right initial awe of Caesar's greatness. In order not to make his personality dominate the play, Shakespeare must play him down and, without destroying his legend, reveal him not as godlike but as a man subject to other men's weaknesses.

Here, we touch on one of Shakespeare's major difficulties. In discussing English history, he could rely on his audience's knowing a good deal about the events of the past 250 years, for the reigns of the kings since Edward III were associated with heroic or terrible events still often recalled in religious, political, and imaginative writings. Most of the barons in the plays from *Henry VI* to *Henry IV* were ancestors, direct or collateral, of Elizabethan nobles, and their family legends were widely known. The great battles of the past, the exiles, usurpations, murders, and intrigues . . . were common knowledge. No such acquaintance with the details of Roman history could be assumed among the citizens who came to see Julius Caesar killed in the Capitol. Shakespeare himself could not have extracted from Plutarch . . . or other authorities so clean an idea of the complex issues involved as [has been] given to modern students. . . . He seems to have wished to compose an objective and impartial picture of the interrelationships among Brutus and Cassius, Caesar, Antony and Octavius, while entering as little as possible into the complexities of the political situation. He was forced to simplify, to depart from Plutarch, not only to avoid bewildering the spectators with recondite allusions but also in order to treat the main characters with evenhanded justice and divided sympathy.

To expiate on Caesar's past exploits and the reforms that as dictator he was planning for Rome, his acts of generosity (including his honoring of his late enemy Brutus) would be to make Brutus into the criminal that Dante thought him. On the other hand, the assassination of Caesar, the strong ruler who had brought order out of chaos, must not seem a virtuous act. Shakespeare was no republican but a defender of the Tudor monarchy, which had brought peace out of civil war and was always afraid of a relapse. Yet in following Plutarch's portrait of Brutus and making him a noble sinner, an altruistic murderer, the dramatist must not give tangible proof that Brutus's suspicions of Caesar's intentions were wrong.

Hence, Shakespeare walks a tightrope in depicting the two chief antagonists—and succeeds by ignoring particular political issues. We do not see Caesar insulting the Senate, and we are not reminded of his egoistic actions, sins against tradition, or love affairs (even Cleopatra is not mentioned); but he is viewed well on this side of idolatry and portrayed as a lover of pomp and circumstance whose tragedy is less ambition than a self-conscious arrogance not justified by the physical or mental qualities shown in the play. We see him patronizing his followers and now displaying bland indifference to warnings that we know have fatal significance, now vacillating (like any mediocre husband) between uxoriousness and public duty. . . . Caesar perishes through a false sense of security, an assurance that misjudges the situation and the men around him. We should not believe all that the envious Cassius and Casca say against him, but some of it strikes home during the first two acts. The balance is adjusted, however, by the assassination and Antony's use of it. With his death, Caesar becomes a martyr, once more the Caesar of popular legend.

Similarly, Brutus might easily in his crucial soliloquy (Act II, Scene 1) have mentioned several ill-boding signs of antirepublican ambition in Caesar's behavior since crossing the Rubicon. Instead, Shakespeare makes him admit:

> Th' abuse of greatness is when it disjoins
> Remorse from power; and, to speak truth of
>   Caesar,
> I have not known when his affections swayed
> More than his reason.
>   —lines 18–21

His decision to join the conspiracy is founded on the supposition that if crowned, Caesar would change his nature ("Then lest he may, prevent"). In depriving Brutus of any substantial reason for the assassination, Shakespeare distorts the historic situation and illustrates the lack of judgment that marks Brutus's character throughout the play. His tragedy, therefore, is that of a man of the noblest moral principles whose idealism blinds him to the realities of politics and to the nature of his fellow conspirators and of the Roman populace. The good man is led to perform an act of murderous injustice. Caesar is killed undeservedly on a presupposition of what he might become; but his story is not ended with his death. "We all stand up against the spirit of Caesar," says Brutus (Act II, Scene 1, line 167), meaning the autocratic ambition of Cae-

sar. But the spirit of Caesar lives on in Antony and Octavius and finally conquers. Moreover, by transforming Brutus's "evil spirit" or "genius" into Caesar's ghost, Shakespeare makes the Battle of Philippi a personal triumph for the dead man as well as for his avengers. . . .

Julius Caesar is a play about a triple group relationship—with Caesar at the center of one group; Brutus, of another; Antony, of the third—and of their interaction in a great conflict that involves the fate of Rome. . . . Shakespeare does not explore the political principles involved; he refers little to the horrors of the Pompeian Wars, . . . and he neither prophesies the strike that followed Philippi nor treats what happens as part of a divinely ordained movement from republic to monarchy. The play lacks the overt didacticism of the English histories. Its emphasis is not on political theory but on the traits of individual men as shown in their public connections.

The play is not a "problem play" in the sense that we are left undecided how to regard the characters. The ambivalence of presentation is not intended to confuse or offer alternative interpretations. We are meant to accept both sides as true to life and to modulate from approval to disapproval, as Plutarch himself did in his *Lives*. For what Shakespeare learned from Plutarch was to represent more clearly than before the paradoxes of human motive, the mixture of good and evil in the same person. The heroic Caesar may be pompous . . . ; the sensual Antony may achieve nobility; the stoic Brutus be tetchy with his friend. In *Julius Caesar* the dramatist achieves a somewhat detached tolerance in his attitude toward historical figures and, at the same time, a critical attitude toward politics and those who take part in it. The romantic hero worship of *Henry V* has given place to a shrewd look at the inner weaknesses of public men. But the mood is still benevolent, and the ancient world has a certain grandeur.

From "*Julius Caesar* and Plutarch" (retitled "A Tragic Chronicle") from *Narrative and Dramatic Sources of Shakespeare* by Geoffrey Bullough. Copyright © 1964 by *Columbia University Press*. Reprinted by permission of the publisher.

"When the Heavens Rain Down Fire"
from Rhetoric in Ancient Rome

by **Anne Barton**

On the eve of Caesar's assassination, when the heavens rain down fire and Rome is filled with prodigies and portents, Casca encounters Cicero in the streets. Breathless and dismayed, Casca pours out a tale of marvels, abnormalities that, he believes, must prefigure some calamity to the state.

Cicero, who remains icily calm, admits that

> Indeed, it is a strange-disposèd time:
> But men may construe things after their
>   fashion,
> Clean from the purpose of the things
>   themselves.
> —Act I, Scene 3, lines 33–35

For Elizabethans, this warning of how language may misrepresent fact, how words—whether involuntarily or on purpose—can falsify experience, must have seemed especially striking on the lips of Cicero: acknowledged grandmaster of the art of persuasion, the greatest orator and rhetorician of the ancient world. Shakespeare's Cicero makes no attempt himself to interpret the terrors of the night. He rests content with the neutral observation that disturbed skies such as these are not to walk in, then leaves the stage. In the very next moment, Cassius enters, and Casca finds himself confronting a man who proceeds at once to construe things "clean from the purpose of the things themselves" and, what is more, makes Casca believe him. By the end of the scene, Casca has not only accepted Cassius's very different view of the tempest as a reflection of the diseased and monstrous condition of Rome under Caesar's rule; he has agreed as a result to join the conspirators and end that rule through an act of violence. In doing so, he helps to bring about precisely that cataclysm, that condition of anarchy and upheaval that, initially, he feared.

Although Cicero has no part in the action of *Julius Caesar,* it seems to have been important to Shakespeare that the audience should, from time to time, be reminded of his presence and of the controversy associated with his name. In the second scene of Act I, Cicero passes across the stage twice as a member of Caesar's entourage. Brutus as bystander remarks on the discontent in his eyes. Casca says that after Antony's abortive effort to crown Caesar, Cicero spoke in Greek and that those who understood him smiled and shook their heads. In Act II, after the scene with Casca, Cicero's name is introduced again when Brutus insists upon overruling his confederates and excluding him from the conspiracy on the highly suspect grounds that "he will never follow anything/That other men begin" (Scene 1, lines 151–152). At Sardis, in Act IV, Cassius is shocked to learn that Cicero was one of the senators proscribed by the triumvirs and that he is dead. It is a scattered collection of references but, I believe, purposeful. By keeping the enormous memory of Cicero alive in his tragedy, Shakespeare constantly directs his audience's attention toward Rome as the city of orators and rhetoricians: a place where the art of persuasion was cultivated, for better or for worse, to an extent unparalleled in any other society. . . .

In *Julius Caesar* the art of persuasion has come to permeate life so completely that people find themselves using it not only to influence others but to deceive themselves. This is true, above all, of Brutus. Brutus is competent enough as a public orator, although he lacks the fire and subtlety of Mark Antony, but his real verbal ingenuity declares itself only when he is using the techniques of oratory to blind himself and (occasionally) his friends. In the orchard soliloquy of Act II, Brutus extracts purpose and resolve not from the fact of the situation but from a collection of verbal nothings: from words like *may* and *would*. There is no tangible basis for Brutus's fears of Caesar. Indeed, as he admits, observation and circumstance suggest the contrary. He is driven, as a result, to do the thing for which he secretly longs—kill Caesar—purely on the basis of a grammatical construction: a verbal emptiness that pretends to have the status of a fact. "Then lest he may, prevent" (Act II, Scene 1, line 28). Antony had said of Caesar earlier in the play that his words were precisely equivalent to deeds: "When Caesar says, 'Do this,' it is performed" (Act I, Scene 2, line 10). Brutus too tries to blur the distinction between speech and action, but the effect he creates is one of self-delusion rather than power.

Shakespeare's Caesar likes to refer to himself in the third person. "Speak; Caesar is turned to hear," he says to the soothsayer in Act I, Scene 2, and in later scenes he resorts to this kind of self-naming almost obsessively. Shakespeare knew, of course, that the historical Caesar had written his commentary on the Gallic Wars in the third person, but there is more behind the mannerism (with Caesar as with General de Gaulle in our own time) than a mere literary practice. Self-naming implies taking oneself very seriously. It is a deliberately grand way of regarding one's own identity, as though that identity were already matter for historians. Antony is never guilty of it in *Julius Caesar*. He delivers all of his great oration in the first person. Brutus, by contrast, not only employs this peculiarly Roman form of the royal "we" in his defense to the citizens; he uses the third person repeatedly in private conversation. "Brutus," he tells Cassius, "had rather be a villager/Than to repute himself a son of Rome/Under these hard conditions . . ." (Act I, Scene 2, line 174). The effect of these persistent presentations of Brutus by Brutus as a somehow externalized object is to suggest that although this man is in many ways noble, he is also far too aware of the fact. Indeed, it suggests an underlying affinity with Caesar: the man Brutus kills, supposedly, because Caesar was ambitious.

Drama Study Guide: The Tragedy of Julius Caesar

Cassius plays upon this failing. His persuasion is as deadly as it is because it recognizes and takes advantage of a deeply buried jealousy of Caesar lurking behind all of Brutus's avowed republican principles, a jealousy that happens to be less conscious than his own. He harps upon Brutus as public figure, the cynosure of every eye whose ancestors drove the kings from Rome: a man whose scope and potentialities for greatness have somehow been cabined, cribbed, confined by the rival presence of Caesar. He makes Brutus feel that he must commit a spectacular public act in order to validate his name. In doing this, Cassius is less than honest. His victim, however, not only plays into his hands but betters his instruction.

In the orchard soliloquy of Act II, Brutus turned the techniques of oratory against his own conscience. He continues to do this throughout the remainder of the play. The man who pretends, in Act IV, that he does not know about his wife's death purely in order to impress Messala with the superhuman fortitude of the hero encountering pain also tries to delude himself that the conspiracy is a kind of holy league. This is why he refuses to countenance an oath to bind its members. Even worse, he uses language dishonestly (much as Othello does after him) when he tries to persuade the conspirators that Caesar's death will be not a butchery but a religious sacrifice:

> We all stand up against the spirit of Caesar,
> And in the spirit of men there is no blood.
> O, that we then could come by Caesar's spirit,
> And not dismember Caesar!
> —Act II, Scene 1, lines 167–170

They must, he claims, be "called purgers, not murderers." The names make all the difference.

In the event, the spirit of Caesar is precisely the thing they do not kill. They merely release it from the shackles of its human form and failings. No longer deaf, arrogant, epileptic, or subject to error, this spirit walks abroad as a thing against which, now, there is no defense. At Philippi it turns the swords of the conspirators into their own proper entrails. It raises up a successor in the form of Octavius, who will annihilate the republic in Rome. Even before this happens, Brutus's appeal to the transforming power of words has become half-desperate. In the spirit of men, there is no blood. But blood, in the first scene of Act III, is the element in which the conspirators are drenched. It dyes all of them scarlet, sticks to hands as well as to daggers, disgustingly daubs their faces and their clothes. Not even Brutus can pretend not to notice the sheer physical mess. Characteristically, he tries to spiritualize it, to alter its character by linguistic means:

> . . . Stoop, Romans, stoop,
> And let us bathe our hands in Caesar's blood
> Up to the elbows, and besmear our swords.
> Then walk we forth, even to the market place,
> And waving our red weapons o'er our heads,
> Let's all cry "Peace, freedom, and liberty!"
> —Act III, Scene 1, lines 105–110

Blood is not blood, he insists, but purely symbolic. It stands for the idea of freedom. The euphemism, and the action with which it is connected, is one of which the second half of the twentieth century has heard all too much.

From "Rhetoric in Ancient Rome" by Anne Barton (retitled "When the Heavens Rain Down Fire") from *Shakespeare's Craft: Eight Lectures,* edited by Philip H. Highfill, Jr. Copyright © 1982 by The George Washington University. Reprinted by permission of *Southern Illinois University Press.*

Elements of the Play

Key Literary Elements of the Play

Note that Brutus is designated the play's protagonist because he comes closest to an Aristotelian tragic hero. If *protagonist* is taken in its general sense, as the character who drives the action, *Julius Caesar* has more than one protagonist. Brutus and Cassius drive the action until Antony's oration, after which Antony emerges as the protagonist.

Protagonist: Brutus

Antagonists: Caesar, Antony, Octavius

Conflicts: person versus person, person versus self

Significant Techniques: blank verse; dramatic, situational, and verbal irony; soliloquy; figurative language; imagery; foreshadowing

Setting: Rome, 44 B.C.; Sardis and Philippi, 42 B.C.

Cast of Characters in the Play

Main Characters

JULIUS CAESAR is a conquering Roman general, a mighty soldier swayed by superstition.

MARCUS BRUTUS is the only conspirator in the plot to assassinate Caesar whose motives are essentially pure. His high sense of idealism is used by Caesar's envious enemies to further their own selfish purposes. Even his enemy, Antony, calls him "the noblest Roman of them all."

MARCUS ANTONIUS (usually called **MARK ANTONY** in the play) sets himself the goal of avenging Caesar's death. His shrewd and wily manipulations are paralleled by Brutus's lofty but shortsighted idealism.

M. AEMILIUS LEPIDUS, though he becomes one of the ruling triumvirs, together with Octavius Caesar and Mark Antony, is "a slight man" who is exploited by his stronger partners.

CASSIUS displays the greed and envy that motivate most of the conspirators. His "itching palms" present a striking contrast to Brutus's basic nobility.

CASCA, another conspirator in the plot against Caesar, hates the ordinary citizenry yet is jealous when the people acclaim Caesar.

OCTAVIUS CAESAR, Julius Caesar's heir, joins with Antony and Lepidus to lead forces against Brutus and to share with them the title of triumvir.

Supporting Characters

ARTEMIDORUS OF CNIDOS, a rhetorician

DECIUS BRUTUS, a conspirator in the plot against Caesar

CALPHURNIA, wife of Caesar

YOUNG CATO, a friend of Brutus's and Cassius's

CICERO, a senator

METELLUS CIMBER, a conspirator in the plot against Caesar

CINNA, a conspirator in the plot against Caesar

CINNA, a poet

CLAUDIUS, a servant of Brutus's

CLITUS, a servant of Brutus's

DARDANIUS, a servant of Brutus's

FLAVIUS, a tribune

LIGARIUS, a conspirator in the plot against Caesar

LUCILIUS, a friend of Brutus's and Cassius's

LUCIUS, a servant of Brutus's

MARULLUS, a tribune

MESSALA, a friend of Brutus's and Cassius's

PINDARUS, a servant of Cassius's

POPILIUS LENA, a senator

PORTIA, wife of Brutus

PUBLIUS, a senator

STRATO, a servant of Brutus's

TITINIUS, a friend of Brutus's and Cassius's

*Drama Study Guide: **The Tragedy of Julius Caesar***

TREBONIUS, a conspirator in the plot against Caesar

VARRO, a servant of Brutus's

VOLUMNIUS, a friend of Brutus's and Cassius's

Also a **SOOTHSAYER, ANOTHER POET, SENATORS, CITIZENS, GUARDS, ATTENDANTS, MESSENGERS**

The Themes of the Play

As students read *Julius Caesar,* encourage them to think about how these themes are parts of Shakespeare's concern:

1. Chaos results when the prescribed social order is overturned.
2. The best intentions of good, noble men can lead to tragedy.
3. Language is a powerful weapon, and in the hands of a skilled person it can be used to manipulate others.
4. Violence and bloodshed can never have morally good results.
5. Orderliness and a stable rule, even though dictatorial, are preferable to social chaos.

A Tragic Plot

Tragic figures are not always totally admirable and heroic, and the more they appear to be ordinary men and women, the more we become aware of certain faults and flaws that explain their fall, at least in part. At the center of a tragic story stands a man or a woman who is a puzzle of character. Though some aspects of character and position make him or her seem greater than most others and therefore heroic, at the same time we are aware of something that makes this person vulnerable. This something is generally a flaw in either outlook or character, a flaw that causes the hero to make some terrible mistake, some disastrous choice, perhaps for the best of reasons. It is this choice that invites some kind of hostile reaction on the part of a power that turns against the hero and asserts its greater strength by frustrating or defeating him or her. Once this choice has been made, a chain of unavoidable consequences follows. Each link in the chain of circumstances seems to limit and confine the hero further, until at last this person is unable to prevent his or her own destruction.

Brutus is an example of this kind of tragic hero. Brutus is caught between two forces, two systems of values, each of which seems to exclude the other. High-minded, idealistic, and committed to freedom, he believes that to live with tyranny is to allow a wrong to be perpetuated. But he also knows that to murder Caesar is to commit a wrong. After much struggle he decides that the murder of Caesar is a holy duty. The irony here is that Brutus's idealism brings to Rome only anarchy and the horrors of civil war, not the peace, freedom, and liberty he had envisioned. But as with all tragic figures, it is very difficult to make simple moral judgments about Brutus. On the one hand, Brutus has a strong sense of being right and can present powerful arguments to justify his action. On the other hand, his passionate sense of integrity can appear to be more a matter of willful pride or a perverse death wish than a moral principle. It comes down to which point of view of him we take. Though mutually exclusive, both views of Brutus are valid.

In Jean Anouilh's version of the tragedy *Antigone,* the chorus says, "Nothing is in doubt and everyone's destiny is known." This sense of the inevitable liberates tragic characters from everyday concerns and frees them to speak with special authority because they have no personal advantages to gain. This is what makes tragedy seem "kingly." This is what, somewhat unexpectedly perhaps, exhilarates and exalts the tragic characters and the audience, for it frees them from the immediate fear of life and, at least for a time, allows them to "be themselves."

*Drama Study Guide: **The Tragedy of Julius Caesar***

Who Is the Hero of the Play?

Readers of *The Tragedy of Julius Caesar* may have difficulty deciding which character in the play is the true hero. In particular, after Caesar is killed, audience involvement is so divided that no single hero emerges. Shakespeare is not wholly sympathetic to Caesar, the conspirators, or Antony.

To the Elizabethans, **Julius Caesar,** because of his historical reputation, would have been the "loftiest" man in the play, but here Caesar is shown at the least impressive stage in his career—his final days—and with none of his earlier vigor. Shakespeare has allowed him to appear in only three scenes, and he dies in the first scene of the third act. A public view reveals a man whose capacity to rule has not been impaired and whose genuine love for his country is difficult to question, whereas a private view reveals a man who has severe physical disabilities and is sometimes pompous and something of a tyrant. Caesar also has an irritating sense of superiority, and he has made enemies: The tribunes of the people hate him because of his triumph over Pompey, and Cassius hates him as a man.

To many, however, Caesar is still the hero of the play—but not this Caesar. It is the spirit of Caesar that emerges as the dominant power of the tragedy, and it is against this spirit that the conspirators must fight. It is their tragedy that they fail to perceive where the true strength of Caesar lies. They succeed only in destroying the body of Caesar; his spirit rises up again, stronger and purer, and avenges his death. The ghost of Caesar, appearing right before the battle at Philippi, is a visible symbol of power in the play.

Marcus Brutus is not only a murderer but a murderer of a fatherlike figure. Often regarded as the true hero of the play, he is with us throughout the play—he is the subject of its final eloquence. Brutus's soliloquy at the beginning of Act II is an agonized attempt to reconcile the tyranny he sees with the Caesar he knows and loves. Ultimately Brutus behaves heroically by putting the "general" (Act II, Scene 1, line 12) before his own good. A true idealist, he is universally admired. Even Cassius responds to the nobility of Brutus, who becomes the image of virtue to his co-conspirators. Brutus is certainly motivated by ideals higher than those impelling the jealous Cassius and the political Antony. Brutus suffers, feels, and learns from the tragedy.

But Brutus is so low-key and meditative that he does not show his feelings and so cannot appeal to ours. He is devoted to his country, but he lacks the love for the people that Caesar had and Antony will have. Moreover, after Caesar's death, Brutus demands from the people the same high ideals that he holds and the same sacrifices that he has been willing to make. He asks too much and so loses the sympathy that the people, and that we as readers, might have felt for him.

The conspiracy is conceived and hatched by **Cassius.** Clever enough to work on the "honorable metal" of Brutus, Cassius cannot put the conspiracy in motion unless he can convince his cohorts that a lofty motive is behind it or find a better man than he to lead it. Brutus is the man. Only Brutus can provide the moral elevation and the prestige that the conspiracy needs.

It is impossible to ignore the view that Cassius is primarily motivated by envy—envy of Caesar and envy of the power Caesar holds. This is certainly not heroic. But Cassius is also a hard-thinking man, brave, devoted to Roman freedom, and proud of being a Roman himself. He is, in fact, also motivated by belief in his cause, his genuine conviction that no Roman should be above another. It is this grand passion that gives Cassius his dignity and raises him to the role of hero.

Both Brutus and Cassius are nothing if not complex. It is their tragedy that the coarser nature of Cassius is ultimately dominated by the finer nature of Brutus—to the eventual destruction of both. Brutus's innocence plays into Cassius's hands. But Cassius admires Brutus, and having played so successfully on Brutus's finer feelings, he cannot help allowing Brutus to achieve moral ascendancy over him. After his initial victory over Brutus, he defers to Brutus's moral scruples while knowing this strategy to be wrong. He allows Brutus his way in his ill-advised decision to seek immediate battle at Philippi.

Perhaps these two heroes are not as unalike as they appear to be at first glance. Cassius is more shrewd and more practical, but both conspirators are idealists, and in terms of cunning and political savvy both are babes in the woods compared with Antony.

In this play at least, **Marcus Antonius** is a success story. He is complex, intelligent, and a thrilling orator. No one else adapts to the changing situation as well as he. Antony knows how to unite personal affection with political ambition. But to succeed, he must come to terms with the ambiguities of life, accepting life as it is; Antony makes no sacrifice for a noble ideal. He can be generous, but he lacks the innocence and the disinterestedness of a hero like Hamlet or Brutus. Some critics think he is motivated by self-interest alone.

*Drama Study Guide: **The Tragedy of Julius Caesar***

Teaching the Play

Objectives

1. To gain exposure to Shakespeare's life and work and to Elizabethan stage conventions
2. To improve reading proficiency and expand vocabulary
3. To recognize how the play relates to contemporary life
4. To identify details of plot, setting, and characterization
5. To respond to the play, orally and in writing
6. To identify and define dramatic and poetic techniques

7. To develop creative writing and dramatization skills, including writing a new scene; rewriting a play's ending; composing a journal entry from a character's perspective; updating characters; expanding one episode into a new story or play; conceptualizing a modern-dress production; making directorial decisions; and performing dramatic readings.
8. To develop critical thinking and writing skills, including responding to a critic; writing a compare-and-contrast essay; analyzing characters; using graphic organizers to map dramatic themes; and conducting research on relevant historical events.

Introducing the Play

Shakespearean Drama

Even students who enjoyed *Romeo and Juliet* may be less than enthusiastic about reading *Julius Caesar*. You may hear such protests as "It's history—*ancient* history." Counter such complaints by explaining that the subject of *Julius Caesar* may be history, but *Julius Caesar* is not *a* history; it's a play.

Point out that Shakespeare took his plots from older literature and from history but wrote in order to move and entertain his contemporaries. Playgoers did not crowd the Globe Theater to learn what happened to Caesar; they knew the story. What they responded to, as audiences do today, were Shakespeare's subtle and fascinating characters; his fast-moving, suspenseful plot; his sharp humor; his power to evoke a world with words. Reassure students that *Julius Caesar* is neither didactic nor dated; it is the story of a political murder, an exploration of political, psychological, and moral turmoil that might remind them of some contemporary movies. (Oliver Stone's *JFK* comes to mind.)

Reassure students, too, that all modern readers need help in understanding Shakespeare's language and his literary, topical, and historical allusions. Let them know that they will get the help they need, both from the text and from you. Stress that their initial bewilderment will give way to pleasure as they begin to see the frightening parallels between the murder of Caesar and contemporary political assassinations.

The Five-Part Dramatic Structure

Also prepare students with a discussion of the five-part dramatic structure, corresponding generally (although not absolutely) to the play's five acts. You may want to duplicate for your students the following diagram and definitions.

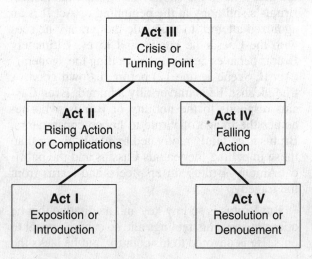

Act III — Crisis or Turning Point

Act II — Rising Action or Complications

Act IV — Falling Action

Act I — Exposition or Introduction

Act V — Resolution or Denouement

Drama Study Guide: The Tragedy of Julius Caesar

The **exposition,** or the **introduction,** establishes tone, setting, some of the main characters, previous events necessary for understanding the play's action, and the main **conflict,** or problem.

The **rising action** is a series of **complications** besetting the protagonist that arise when the protagonist takes action to resolve his or her main conflict.

The **crisis,** or **turning point,** is the moment of choice for the protagonist, the moment when the forces of conflict come together and the situation will either improve or inexorably deteriorate. The crisis usually occurs in Act III.

The **falling action** presents the incidents resulting from the protagonist's decision at the turning point. In tragedy these incidents necessarily emphasize the play's destructive forces but often include an episode of possible salvation, as well as comic scenes. These are the playwright's means of maintaining suspense and relieving the tension as the catastrophe approaches.

The **resolution,** or **denouement,** is the conclusion of the play, the unraveling of the plot, which in tragedy includes the **catastrophe** of the hero's and others' deaths. The **climax,** or emotional peak, usually occurs right before the denouement.

The Appeal of the Play

The Tragedy of Julius Caesar is a play of political intrigue. Its main characters are men of great power whose actions affect thousands and change history. Students should see that these men, like leaders of all times, are not infallible; they are human. Each character in *The Tragedy of Julius Caesar* is an individual possessing a unique temperament and history that color political and moral idealism. Moreover, the characters do not act in isolation; each is inextricably linked with the others. Disagreements produce compromise; one judgment overrules another; unforeseen events force hasty actions. Students should understand that *tragic flaw* is not just a literary term: Good people, through error and temporary weakness, can wreak havoc on themselves and others. In *The Tragedy of Julius Caesar,* the honorable Brutus

joins a conspiracy to murder Caesar, believing that in doing so he is saving Rome from a tyrant. As it turns out, however, his decision has disastrous consequences. Life is full of difficult decisions, and it is not always easy to discern whether a choice is based on the proper motives. Students will almost certainly understand the moral ambiguity implicit in such a choice.

Begin by asking students for a definition of the word *honor,* and write their responses on the chalkboard. Have them provide examples of honorable behavior, either from their personal experiences or from television shows, books, or movies. Ask the following questions: Do you agree with the ideal of honor portrayed by the media? Is there such a thing as an absolute standard of honor that applies to everyone? Is honor an inherent quality in an individual, or is it something that is created and shaped by experience? Next, explore meanings of the word *ambition,* and have students give examples of ambition as a positive or a negative force.

Encourage students to provide examples of times when they, someone they know, someone in history or contemporary life, or a fictional character has had to choose between honor and ambition. What choices did these people make? What consequences did they face as a result of their choices? How might the situation have been resolved had an alternative course of action been chosen?

In particular, have students discuss how often revolution, assassination, abuses of power, and bloody battles occur in contemporary life and how often powerful oratory and propaganda stir the masses. (This latter scenario is all too relevant today.) If students consider the human dramas behind recent revolutions as well as those behind the revolutions in America and France in the eighteenth century, they may be surprised by the immediacy of Shakespeare's story. They will see that this has happened again and again in history. To reinforce the play's immediacy, you might direct students to John Mason Brown's review of a 1937 production of *Julius Caesar,* which was set in a fascist country that resembled Hitler's Germany. (See pages 140–144 of the HRW Classics edition of *Julius Caesar.*)

Reading and Performing the Play

Some teachers like to plunge their students immediately into a brief "performance" of the play. If you want to try this, assign parts for an informal performance of Act I, Scene 1, the crowd scene. All students will be familiar with contemporary

parallels to this scene: A crowd of workers awaits the arrival of a popular military hero. Two politicians of the opposite stripe try to disperse the crowd. One worker acts like a wise guy with the politicians.

Drama Study Guide: ***The Tragedy of Julius Caesar***

Don't have a rehearsal; just get four students up in front of the class, books in hand, and have them read their parts. (You might want to have another half dozen students act as the crowd: They don't speak but just mill about.) Unless your class is especially small, you can probably have several groups take turns performing the scene. You'll undoubtedly be surprised at how quickly the students will catch on to what's happening in Rome and how quickly, with a few of these impromptu performances, some of the hurdles to the language will have been cleared.

When you assign the reading of Act I, go over the format of the text carefully. Show students that unfamiliar words, phrases, and allusions are marked with a symbol and explained in a footnote that is keyed to the appropriate number. Next, read a few of the Guided Reading questions provided for you on page 32 of this guide. Explain that these questions aid understanding by pointing to details of the plot and eliciting interpretations of character, language, and staging.

Use the first class period after students have read the act to allow them to *hear* Shakespeare's language. Read the opening scene yourself, play a recording, or show a film. This will provide a model of correct phrasing as well as show how much an actor's interpretation adds to the play's meaning.

A resource that is full of good ideas about teaching the play by means of performance is the Folger Library's *Shakespeare Set Free,* edited by Peggy O'Brien (Washington Square Press, published by Pocket Books).

Understanding the Literary Elements

Remind students of the genre they are studying: Drama is a literary *and* a performing art. *Julius Caesar,* though written to be acted, is splendid reading. As you read, play recordings, and show films, students should see how gestures, timing, staging, sound effects, and actors' interpretations can affect meaning. Although the words do not change from performance to performance, the audience's perceptions and reactions do. The questions and exercises in this Study Guide will help students appreciate Shakespeare's mastery of dramatic structure and literary techniques. By reading and studying this play, students should come to see how Shakespeare keeps the audience's interest—how he alternates scenes of psychological subtlety with emotional peaks, such as Caesar's murder, Antony's oration, and the quarrel between Brutus and Cassius. They should also come to see that Antony's eloquence is Shakespeare's eloquence: In his oration, Antony uses exquisite verse, subtle

irony, evocative imagery, and vivid figures of speech to move his listeners—Shakespeare does this throughout the play.

Establishing a Procedure

Before you begin to teach *Julius Caesar,* examine the teaching resources in this Study Guide; they provide a wealth of ideas for classroom work, homework assignments, projects, reports, and tests. If possible, obtain a film of *Julius Caesar,* as well as books and audiovisual materials about Shakespeare, his times, and the Globe Theater. (Check with your school or public library for the availability of the BBC television production and the MGM film of the play.) Then, determine which projects and writing exercises you will assign at the beginning of the unit, decide how you will present each act, and prepare a daily reading and assignment schedule. If possible, allow four weeks for the study of the play.

Use the first two or three days for preparation. Discuss the Introduction to the HRW Classics edition of *Julius Caesar* (pages 1–14), and enhance the historical information with filmstrips, films, or illustrated books. Do not let students be intimidated by the poetry of the play; introduce terms and read passages aloud but delay scrutiny of the dramatic technique until they are interested in the play and more comfortable with its language. In the same way, briefly introduce the five-part structure of Shakespearean drama. In doing this, you are providing students with a vocabulary for discussing form, which they will do with much more understanding as they follow the plot.

Finally, distribute your schedule for the play, and explain long-range projects and writing exercises. For example, if you want the class to undertake small-group activities, you should assign students to groups at this point so that they can begin working together.

Here is a suggested procedure for presenting each act of the play. Before students begin reading, establish the time and place of each scene (if you desire, summarize the plot or distribute a plot summary); assign vocabulary words, discussion questions, and any writing exercises; designate passages for oral reading; alert students to any scenes of which you will play a recording; and remind students about quizzes and scheduled project reports.

Schedule at least two days of class time for each act, with the exception of Act III, which will require three days. Vary activities from act to act as much as possible. The suggested combination of oral readings, discussion, viewings of scenes, and project reports should keep students stimulated throughout the course of the play.

Drama Study Guide: The Tragedy of Julius Caesar

After students finish reading the play, show a filmed production straight through; students will by then know the play very well, and the viewing will synthesize their experience of its elements.

Providing for Different Levels of Ability

Work individually with students who have particular difficulty with Shakespeare's language, and emphasize paraphrasing in both written and oral work. To prepare students with limited English, have them make full use of plot summaries, vocabulary definitions, and audiovisual aids in conjunction with small-group projects and writing exercises.

Additional options for teaching the play are described, act by act, beginning below.

Options for Teaching the Play

Use these ideas to modify your instruction to suit the needs of individual students.

Act I

Strategies for Inclusion

ENGLISH LANGUAGE DEVELOPMENT   To ensure that students are comprehending the text, frequent check tests may be necessary. As students read the text, ask them to stop at various intervals and to take their focus off the page before answering these questions.

1. Who is speaking?
2. What is the character speaking about?
3. To whom is the character speaking?

LESS PROFICIENT READERS   When you assign the reading of Act I, go over the format of the text carefully. Show students that unfamiliar words, phrases, and allusions are marked with a symbol and explained in a footnote keyed to the appropriate line number. Read a few of the Guided Reading questions, and explain that these questions aid understanding by checking plot details and eliciting interpretations of character, language, theme, and staging. Suggest to students that they first read each scene straight through, using the footnotes to aid their comprehension, and that they then return to the Guided Reading questions, which will stimulate their thought and enhance their appreciation.

AUDITORY   To provide a model of correct phrasing and to show students how much an actor's interpretation adds to meaning, read the opening scene aloud, play a recording, or show a film. Check with your school or public library for the availability of productions of the play on film or videotape.

Integrating the Language Arts

STRATEGIC READING   To encourage interaction with the play and to help students develop a method of critical reading, have them keep dialect or double-entry journals. As students read the play, have them copy, on the left side of a piece of paper, lines or quotations from the play that they find particularly significant or meaningful. On the right side of the paper, have students respond, question, make personal connections, evaluate, or interpret the selected passage. At the end of each act, have each student share a journal entry with the class. *Remind students to choose a situation they would not mind sharing with others.*

WRITING: SOLILOQUY   Remind students that a soliloquy is the act of talking to oneself, and as a dramatic convention the character speaking reveals private thoughts to the audience. Ask them to re-read Cassius's soliloquy at the end of Scene 2 and to write a soliloquy that Brutus might have spoken simultaneously.

Classroom Management

BASE GROUPS   To help students master Shakespeare's language, understand the play's plot line, and analyze the themes of *Julius Caesar,* assign them to base groups—cooperative learning groups that will remain intact throughout the teaching of this play. Ideally, groups should be teacher chosen, composed of students with mixed ability levels, and limited to four or fewer students. As students work on assigned vocabulary, paraphrase passages, or answer discussion questions, individuals may need help, and they will benefit from consultation with their base group.

Crossing the Curriculum

MUSIC   As a long-term project, have students work in groups to locate recorded music that creates an appropriate mood for each act of the play.

Remind them to review the major events in each act so that they can identify music that reflects the atmosphere of the act. Have them share their musical selections with the class and explain why they chose them.

ARCHITECTURE Encourage students to research the guiding principles of classic Roman architecture. On a piece of poster board, they should draw or cut and paste pictures of Roman architecture from the classical period. They may then give a brief oral presentation on their findings.

Problem Solving/Critical Thinking

THE ART OF PERSUASION In this act, students see Cassius cunningly manipulate and flatter Brutus to persuade him to contemplate joining the conspiracy. Divide the class into groups, and ask students to come up with a hypothetical situation in which one group uses manipulative tactics to persuade another to undertake an activity. An appropriate example might be students in one group attempting to persuade those in another to participate in a talent show. Then, have students role-play the situation for the class. The persuaders should use the same persuasive tactics that Cassius employs with Brutus. The students who are being persuaded should contemplate the benefits and drawbacks of each argument and list examples of each on the chalkboard.

Assessment Tools

CHECK TEST: QUESTIONS AND ANSWERS

1. In the opening scene, what two events are the workers celebrating? [They are celebrating the feast of Lupercal and Caesar's defeat of Pompey.]
2. During the celebration, what warning does the soothsayer give to Caesar? [He warns Caesar to beware the ides of March.]
3. Who does Caesar feel is dangerous? [He feels Cassius is dangerous.]
4. What does Casca report that Mark Antony did after the Lupercal games? [Antony offered Caesar a crown.]
5. At the end of the act, how is Cassius planning to win Brutus to the conspiracy? [He has written anonymous letters to Brutus and plans to visit him at home.]

INFORMAL ASSESSMENT Be aware of whether students are using the language of the play to respond to questions and to participate in class discussion. Rate their performance on a scale of one to five (five points being the best), using the following three criteria:

1 Students use important words from the play (that is, theme words).
2 Students quote lines from the play when appropriate.
3 Students use citations correctly.

Act II

Strategies for Inclusion

AUDITORY Explain to students that when they are reading a play, reading aloud or acting out the scenes is a helpful technique because often it will help them hear the tone of the dialogue. Read some scenes aloud; then, have students take turns reading selected scenes aloud. Assign reading parts ahead of time so students may practice before reading in class.

LESS PROFICIENT READERS To focus students' attention on significant ideas and facts in the play, provide a limited number of preview questions to be answered as students read Act II. Questions should be limited to the most pertinent facts and concepts and presented in order of appearance in the selection. It may be helpful for you to write each question on a separate card and clip it to the page on which it appears in the text.

Integrating the Language Arts

STRATEGIC READING Pair each student with a partner, and have pairs read a scene from the play. One student should ask the other questions that come to mind about the reading. The second student should answer as many questions as possible. Students should then reverse roles, with the second student asking the questions and the first answering them. To conclude, ask one student in each pair to summarize what he or she understands so far.

SPEAKING AND LISTENING After students have had practice reading the play aloud, have them prepare a dramatic reading of a soliloquy or a monologue. A dramatic reading involves using tone of voice, gestures, and facial expressions to convey the meaning of the text. Students should stand in front of the class and perhaps read from the text as they perform.

Drama Study Guide: The Tragedy of Julius Caesar

WRITING: DIARY ENTRY Have students write one diary entry assuming the persona of Brutus and one entry assuming the character of Cassius. Diary entries should reveal the character's inner feelings about the conspiracy, Caesar, and the events in Act II. Be sure students include at least two quotations from the play.

Cooperative Learning

ANALYZE DIFFICULT LINES As they read through Act II, ask students to note lines they find difficult to comprehend. After they have finished reading the act, have students work in groups to share their notes with the other group members. Group members may work together to analyze lines for meaning and interpretation.

Crossing the Curriculum

ART Have students illustrate with a painting or a drawing the scene described by Calphurnia in Scene 2, lines 13–26. Remind them that this passage recounts Calphurnia's sighting of supernatural events in the streets of Rome. Display students' artwork in the classroom as a visual reinforcer.

GEOGRAPHY To give students a better idea of the size of the ancient Roman Empire and the expansion of Roman territories during Caesar's life, have them trace a map of Europe and label the principal cities of Italy and the other Roman territories. They may find encyclopedias and historical maps helpful in their work on this project.

HEALTH In this act, students see Calphurnia deeply disturbed about a dream and its possible interpretation. Since ancient times, people have been fascinated by the mysterious quality of dreams.

Have students work in groups to do research and write short reports on the history of dream interpretation.

Assessment Tools

CHECK TEST: TRUE-FALSE

1. At home alone Brutus initially decides that Caesar should not die but changes his mind after Cassius arrives. [False]
2. After the conspirators leave, Brutus refuses to tell Portia what is troubling him despite her pleas. [False]
3. On the morning of March 15, Calphurnia persuades Caesar to stay home, but when Decius reinterprets her dream, Caesar decides to go to the Senate. [True]
4. Artemidorus knows about the murder plot but is afraid to warn Caesar. [False]
5. Portia meets the soothsayer, who is waiting near the Capitol to warn Caesar again of danger. [True]

ONGOING ASSIGNMENT To check students' reading comprehension and to encourage students to reflect on what they have read, have them respond near the end of each class period to one of the following questions or to other reflective questions that you devise. Select different students to read their responses each day.

- So far, do you like this work? Why or why not?
- What do you think is the most important word, phrase, or passage in this work? Why?
- Are there any parts of this work that are confusing to you? Which parts? Why?
- If you were an English teacher, would you teach this work to your class? Why or why not?

Act III

Strategies for Inclusion

INTERPERSONAL Remind students that Act III contains the play's turning point—the pivotal moment when the hero's fortunes begin to decline, setting in motion the play's falling action, which leads to its inevitable catastrophe. As they read, ask students to decide which event or decision constitutes this turning point. After the class has read the act, give pairs of students a self-adhesive note. Instruct each pair to mark the turning point by affixing the note next to the appropriate lines. Have students defend their choices to the class.

LEARNERS HAVING DIFFICULTY To ensure that all students understand why Antony's funeral speech is an example of persuasive writing at its most effective, discuss ahead of time such persuasive devices as specific evidence, verbal irony, loaded words, repetition, and appeals to self-interest or emotions. Have students work in groups to identify Antony's use of these devices in his speech.

SPECIAL NEEDS Guided reading activities are some of the best ways in which to help all students understand the text. Passages for which you will

Drama Study Guide: The Tragedy of Julius Caesar

want to use guided reading include Antony's famous speech, which begins on line 75 of Scene 2 and continues with interruptions through line 254. Read aloud, pausing after an important sentence or a key idea to ask questions and discuss what has just been said.

LESS PROFICIENT READERS Before students begin reading this pivotal act, review the format for recording a reference to a particular line so that they will be able to refer properly to lines and scenes in their discussions and writing. Familiarity with this technique will allow them to take notes more quickly and easily. Review the way in which lines are counted. Point out that in split lines the number appears only once even though the line includes the speech of two characters. Note that in this edition, acts are represented by capital Roman numerals and line numbers are written in Arabic numerals. The act number always appears first, the scene number second, and the line number(s) third.

Integrating the Language Arts

STRATEGIC READING To encourage students to examine events and speculate about their long-range consequences, have them stop at the end of Scene 1 and write a prediction journal entry. Ask them to divide a sheet of paper in half lengthwise and record on the left side "What Happened" in Scene 1. On the right side, have them write "What Might Happen as a Result of This." Discuss students' predictions with the class. After students have read Scene 2, ask them to return to their predictions and compare their forecasts with what actually happens.

LANGUAGE AND STYLE Have students compare and contrast the rhetorical style of Brutus's funeral speech with that of Antony's. Ask them to consider the effect of the use of prose as opposed to blank verse, the tone of the two speeches, and the types of rhetorical and persuasive devices employed. Then, have them design posters that graphically compare the two speeches. These posters should also indicate the more effective speech and explain why it is superior.

Cooperative Learning

EXPERT GROUPS In this activity, members of small groups become highly knowledgeable about one aspect of a topic or a literary work and serve as experts. One group might become experts on the Globe Theater, one on Elizabethan English, one on the Aristotelian concept of tragedy, and one on Plutarch's *Life of Caesar*. The groups should then report to the class and answer whatever questions other students have about their areas of expertise.

Crossing the Curriculum

FINE ARTS Have students design four costumes for the play. They may use either Elizabethan or Roman dress, but have them conduct research to authenticate it. They should draw their designs in color and cite the scenes for which they are created.

SOCIAL SCIENCES Stage a philosophical debate in your classroom. Have students take sides on the question, Does history repeat itself? Encourage students to locate events in the play that subsequently were repeated in history. Assign students on each side to smaller groups for developing supporting arguments. Have each group's spokesperson present the group's supporting argument to the class.

Problem Solving/Critical Thinking

DECISION MAKING In this act, Brutus makes a series of fatal decisions that set in motion the play's falling action and lead to his and Cassius's downfall. Have students work in small groups to identify these mistakes and, assuming the persona of Cassius, offer arguments to persuade Brutus to reverse his poor judgment.

Assessment Tools

CRITICAL COMMENT: THE CLIMAX Some critics identify the assassination itself as the turning point of the play; others believe the turning point occurs when Antony returns to the Capitol, plotting revenge; still others believe it is the moment in Antony's funeral oration when the crowd turns on the conspirators. Although Caesar's murder is clearly an emotional climax, it does not in itself ensure the conspirators' downfall; neither does Antony's return after the murder, since there is still the possibility that Cassius's judgment will prevail and Antony will not be allowed to address the crowd. Clearly Antony's speech is also a climax in the play—but one that is beyond the conspirators' control (Brutus is no longer even present). Thus, the speech is a consequence of the turning point rather than the turning point itself.

CHECK TEST: QUESTIONS AND ANSWERS
1. What does Caesar say when he sees the soothsayer? [He says that the ides of March have come.]
2. Who strikes the first and last blows in Caesar's assassination? [Casca strikes first and Brutus last.]

Drama Study Guide: The Tragedy of Julius Caesar

26

HRW MATERIAL COPYRIGHTED UNDER NOTICE APPEARING EARLIER IN THIS WORK.

3. When Antony comes to the Capitol, how does he show the conspirators that he is a friend? [He shakes hands with each one.]

4. When Antony speaks at the funeral, what does he show to the crowd to arouse their emotions? [He shows the crowd Caesar's bloody mantle and wounded corpse.]

5. After leaving the funeral, what does the mob do? [The mob kills Cinna the poet.]

OBSERVATION ASSESSMENT   Use the following checklist as you observe and assess students' participation in class discussion.

3 Always   **2** Sometimes   **1** Rarely

_____ **1.** Actively participates in discussion.

_____ **2.** Articulates responses clearly.

_____ **3.** Listens to what other students say.

_____ **4.** Thinks before speaking.

_____ **5.** Waits to be called on.

_____ **6.** Gives reasons for responses.

Act IV

Strategies for Inclusion

INTERPERSONAL   In Act IV, new insights into the play's main characters are provided. Before beginning the act, have students work in pairs to create a character-attribute cluster for Antony, Brutus, or Cassius. Ask them to add new attributes to the cluster as they gain additional insight into their character in this act.

LESS PROFICIENT READERS   If students experience difficulty with the long and detailed conversation between Brutus and Cassius in Scene 3, try a paired summarizing activity. Have the first student read until the second one calls out "Stop." The second student should then summarize what the first has read. The first student should not interrupt and should ask questions only after the second student has completed the summary. The students should then reverse their roles.

AUDITORY   It is often expedient to arrive at reasons for or against a particular stance by articulating them in an informal debate. Have students work in pairs, and ask each partner to decide which side to take in the following debate: _The conspiracy led by Brutus and Cassius was a force for good._ Turn on an audiocassette recorder, and tape the ensuing debate. Debaters should not initially be preoccupied with the logical soundness of their own arguments, because this is a prewriting activity. A student should make a point, support it with evidence from the drama, and then allow his or her partner to rebut that point and counter with an opposing point. This process should continue until the debaters run out of points. The tape should be replayed, and the debaters may then record valid points for the debate.

Integrating the Language Arts

WRITING: CHARACTER SKETCH   Have students choose one of the main characters in the play and write a brief character sketch. They should use at least three of the following methods to show what their character is like.

• his/her appearance
• his/her actions
• his/her words
• the reactions of others to him/her

LANGUAGE AND STYLE   Have students analyze the following sentences from Act IV to see how Shakespeare's figurative language creates vivid images in the reader's mind. Ask them to answer the questions that follow.

• "But hollow men, like horses hot at hand, / Make gallant show and promise of their mettle. . . ."
• "For I am armed so strong in honesty. . . ."
• "And here my naked breast; within, a heart / Dearer than Pluto's mine, richer than gold"

Answers are presented in the order of the examples above.

1. What figure(s) of speech are used in each? [Simile; metaphor; simile]

2. What image comes to mind when you read each passage? [Battle; battle; precious metals]

3. Why are these comparisons effective? [They all appeal to age-old imagery.]

Cooperative Learning

HOT SEAT   This collaborative activity allows students to pretend to become a character in literature. Divide the class into small groups of three

Drama Study Guide: **The Tragedy of Julius Caesar**

to four students. Each student should choose to portray one of the characters in the story. Have students take turns responding in character to questions posed by other group members. To facilitate implementation of the hot seat, first brainstorm as a whole-class activity to gather possible questions and responses to questions.

DIRECTORS FOR A DAY Divide the class into small groups, and have students imagine that they are directing a production of *Julius Caesar*. Ask them to choose one scene and write directions for characterization, timing, blocking, costuming, and sound effects. Groups should then implement these directions by rehearsing their scenes. Finally, each group might stage its scene for the rest of the class.

Classroom Management

SEEKING VARIED STUDENT RESPONSES To ensure that you solicit a range of responses from different students and avoid falling into the trap of calling on the same few students, try some of the following techniques.

- Keep track of which students contribute and the number of times each contributes.
- Tell students that they must participate a certain number of times, and give a grade for participation.
- Call on students at random by drawing names.
- To elicit different responses, use questions like, What is another solution?
- Reserve judgment when students respond.

Crossing the Curriculum

SOCIAL SCIENCES Both Brutus and Portia adhere to the philosophy of Stoicism. Have students do additional research on Stoicism and report their findings to the class. They may write a paragraph about Stoicism on the chalkboard for the class to copy, or they may present an oral report.

FINE ARTS Have students work with their classmates to write a television script, including stage directions and camera angles, for one of the following scenes: Caesar at home on the morning of March 15; Caesar's assassination; Antony's oration; the ghost's visit to Brutus. If possible, students should perform, videotape, and present the finished scene to the class.

Assessment Tools

OBSERVATION ASSESSMENT As students discuss Acts I through IV of *Julius Caesar*, note whether they are making specific references to echoes and repetitions in the text. The following scale may help you evaluate students' responses.

1 Discusses text generally or inaccurately.
2 Speaks generally, with some mention of lines or scenes.
3 Refers to lines or scenes without citing specific references.
4 Occasionally cites specific references to support discussion.
5 Frequently cites specific references to support discussion.

CHECK TEST: QUESTIONS AND ANSWERS

1. Who are the three men ruling Rome? [Antony, Octavius, and Lepidus are the rulers.]
2. Where are Brutus and Cassius when they meet in Scene 2? [They are near Sardis, in Asia Minor.]
3. What reports about Cassius have angered Brutus? [Cassius is rumored to have taken bribes.]
4. After the two men quarrel, what personal trouble does Brutus reveal to Cassius? [Portia has committed suicide.]
5. What is Brutus and Cassius's final military plan, and who suggests it? [They will engage the triumvirate at Philippi, as Brutus suggests.]

Act V

Strategies for Inclusion

ADVANCED Have interested students compare the historical Julius Caesar with the Shakespearean character. Then, have them use their research to compose a letter from Shakespeare to his audience, defending the changes he made when writing the play.

ENGLISH LANGUAGE DEVELOPMENT To help students stay focused on **plot,** work with them to keep a time line of the actions that take place. Pause periodically with the class to review what has happened in the play.

VISUAL/AUDITORY Have students work in groups of three or four to create a computer-

Drama Study Guide: The Tragedy of Julius Caesar

animated scene with sound. Each group should choose a short portion of a scene from the play and use available technology to make a presentation. One student might find out how the technology works, another might do the artwork, another might plan the animation, and another might create the sound.

Integrating the Language Arts

STRATEGIC READING   To review and reinforce the chronology of the story, divide the class into three or four groups after everyone has finished reading the play. Have one student in each group read or recite a memorable or important line from the play. Other students in the group should try to identify the speaker and the situation in which the line is said. Let students take turns so that everyone will have an opportunity both to read and to guess.

WRITING: CHANGING GENRES   Have students work individually or in small groups to transform a portion of *Julius Caesar* into an excerpt from a novel. Ask them to read their excerpts aloud, and discuss as a class how reading a novel is different from reading a play.

LANGUAGE AND VOCABULARY   After students finish Act V, ask them to return to earlier acts and identify lines that they understand differently now that they are accustomed to Shakespearean language. Ask them to list words that they find have layers of meaning. Then, have them develop some of these key words into collages that show possible interpretations.

Cooperative Learning

FIELDING QUESTIONS   Put up a large sheet of kraft paper on which students may write questions as they read. Have them leave room between questions so that other students may answer their questions. Periodically check to make sure that misconceptions are cleared up. Leave a few minutes at the beginning or end of class to discuss the posted questions and answers or to allow students to add or answer new questions.

Classroom Management

MANAGING THE READER'S RESPONSE CLASSROOM   To encourage students to see that there is not just one way to look at a literary work, allow several students to express their opinions before the class. Encourage them to amend their responses after they have considered the input of others.

Crossing the Curriculum

HISTORY   Have students investigate and report on other failed military strategies. They may look at British tactics in the American Revolution, Napoleon's strategies in Russia, or Hitler's mistakes on the eastern front, for example. Ask them to give an oral report in which they tell the class about the tactical mistakes that were made in a given battle or campaign and show the strategic errors, using a poster or a slide.

FINE ARTS   Have students work in groups of four to create a piece of scenery for the play. The design should reflect a thoughtful interpretation of its role in the play. Assign each student a leadership role: an artist (to direct the painting or drawing), a production manager (to oversee the collection of building materials), a director (to compare the details noted in the play with the group's rendering of the scene), and a stage manager (to consider placement and use of the scenery).

Problem Solving/Critical Thinking

PROBLEM RESOLUTION   In this act both Cassius and Brutus react extremely: Cassius has Pindarus kill him when he mistakenly believes that Brutus's army has been overtaken by Antony's forces, and similarly, Brutus kills himself when he believes he is headed for certain defeat at Philippi after he discovers Cassius's body. Ask students to answer the following question: What are several positive and constructive actions that each of these military leaders could have taken? Students may write their responses in their Reader's Logs and read them aloud if they so desire. Students who find this assignment especially compelling may wish to write a new ending for the play.

Assessment Tools

CHECK TEST: TRUE-FALSE
1. Before the battle, Antony, Octavius, Brutus, and Cassius meet in a tent to shake hands and pledge an honorable fight. [False]
2. During the battle, Pindarus mistakes Brutus's troops for the enemy and reports to Cassius that Titinius is captured. [True]
3. Cassius commits suicide by recklessly going into the battle unarmed. [False]
4. Brutus is captured by Antony and commits suicide out of shame. [False]
5. At the play's end, Antony is the new ruler of Rome. [False]

*Drama Study Guide: **The Tragedy of Julius Caesar***

Plot Synopsis

Act I

In Scene 1, the Roman people are celebrating the feast of Lupercal and Julius Caesar's triumphant return to Rome after his defeat of Pompey's sons. Two tribunes hostile to Caesar chastise a group of commoners for their disloyalty to Pompey, drive them from the streets, and begin removing decorations from the town's statues.

In Scene 2, as Caesar and his retinue walk to the Lupercal games, a soothsayer warns Caesar to beware of the ides of March. Brutus and Cassius remain behind, and when Brutus expresses his fear that the people will crown Caesar king, Cassius tries to persuade Brutus to join a conspiracy against Caesar. Brutus agrees to consider it but does not commit himself. Casca, returning from the games, reports that Mark Antony three times offered Caesar a crown, which he grandly refused before a cheering crowd. Cassius plots to write Brutus anonymous letters praising his honor and hinting at Caesar's dangerous ambition.

At the beginning of Scene 3, it is the night of March 14. Amid storms and portents, Cassius makes final plans to win Brutus to his side. Knowing that opposing senators intend to crown Caesar the next day, Cassius calls together his fellow conspirators, writes further inflammatory letters to Brutus, and sets out to visit him with a last appeal.

Act II

At home before dawn on March 15, Brutus convinces himself that Caesar must die. When Cassius and his faction arrive, Brutus joins the conspiracy but stops Cassius's plan to kill Antony. Portia, who has seen the men come and go, chastises Brutus for not telling her why he is so troubled, and he reluctantly agrees to tell her.

In Scene 2, Caesar is at home early on March 15, planning to go to the Senate even though wild storms and freakish events disturb Rome. Calphurnia has dreamed that Caesar's statue spouts blood, and augurers warn him to stay home. At Calphurnia's pleading he changes his mind about attending the Senate, but Decius Brutus, one of the conspirators, goads him about his weakness, interprets the dream favorably, and reports that the Senate will that day crown him. The other conspirators arrive, and Caesar prepares to accompany them to the Senate.

In Scene 3, Artemidorus, who has written a scroll warning of the plot, stands near the Capitol, hoping to give the scroll to Caesar as he passes.

Act II concludes with Scene 4, in which Portia, greatly disturbed by what Brutus has implied, meets the soothsayer. He tells her that he is waiting to warn Caesar of danger.

Act III

In Scene 1, Caesar discounts the soothsayer's warning and accepts Artemidorus's scroll but does not read it. At the Capitol one conspirator keeps Antony away while the others surround Caesar, urging him to grant Metellus Cimber's petition to end his brother's exile. Caesar refuses the petition, and Casca strikes the first blow of the assassination. Each conspirator stabs Caesar; at the final blow, from Brutus, Caesar cries, *"Et tu, Brutè?"* and dies. Brutus, preparing to address the people, accepts Antony's avowal of allegiance and grants him permission to speak at Caesar's funeral.

In Scene 2, at Caesar's funeral at the forum, Brutus justifies to the people his murderous actions, saying that although he loved Caesar, he loves Rome more. The people accept his explanation; but after he leaves, Antony's masterfully ironic oration convinces them of the conspirators' treachery. After Antony displays Caesar's wounds and reads Caesar's will, the furious mob rushes out to burn the conspirators' houses, driving Brutus and Cassius from the city. Antony goes to meet Octavius, Caesar's grandnephew and legitimate successor, who has come to Rome with Lepidus.

In Scene 3, the mob kills the innocent poet Cinna, believing him to be Cinna the conspirator.

Act IV

In Scene 1, Antony, Octavius, and Lepidus are now ruling Rome as a triumvirate. When Antony and Octavius learn that the exiled Brutus and Cassius have raised armies to challenge them, they move to combine their military forces, recruit more men, and meet the challengers' attack.

At the beginning of Scene 2, Brutus and Cassius meet at a camp near Sardis, in Asia Minor. Each has grievances against the other, but Brutus warns Cassius against arguing in front of the soldiers; they retire to Brutus's tent.

In Scene 3, Brutus upbraids Cassius for rumored bribe taking, denounces him for hoarding gold, and casts doubt on his honor and commitment. Cassius, incensed at Brutus's distrust, denies the charge and counters that Brutus is impractical and inexperienced as a soldier. They quarrel, reconcile, and repledge their commitment, after which Brutus reveals that Portia's suicide is partly responsible for his troubled mind. Meanwhile, Antony and Octavius are advancing toward Philippi, several days' journey from Sardis. Cassius advises that they wait at Sardis in order to exhaust the enemy's forces, but Brutus's plan to march on to Philippi prevails. That night the ghost of Caesar tells Brutus that they will meet again at Philippi.

Act V

In Scene 1, Octavius, Antony, Cassius, and Brutus, meeting on the plains of Philippi, exchange taunts before the battle begins.

In Scene 2, Brutus gains an advantage over Octavius's army and orders reinforcements, confident he can overthrow Octavius with a "sudden push."

Scene 3 opens on another part of the battlefield, where Titinius reports to Cassius that his army is surrounded by Antony's men and that Brutus's soldiers have begun looting. Cassius sends Titinius to determine whether some distant troops are friends or enemies and then asks Pindarus to observe Titinius and report what he sees. Pindarus mistak-enly reports that the enemy has captured Titinius, and Cassius orders Pindarus to kill him. He dies saying that Caesar is avenged. When Titinius, returning with the news of Brutus's victory, sees Cassius dead, he kills himself. Brutus finds both bodies.

In the final scene, Brutus, facing defeat, persuades Strato to hold his sword while he falls on it, and so Brutus dies. Octavius, victorious, ends the fighting by inviting Brutus's followers into his service, and Antony declares Brutus "the noblest Roman of them all."

Drama Study Guide: The Tragedy of Julius Caesar

HRW MATERIAL COPYRIGHTED UNDER NOTICE APPEARING EARLIER IN THIS WORK.

31

Guided Reading

The questions and comments that follow focus on the staging, characterization, and plot development of the play. They ask students for their opinions and their comments and are designed to help them think about and respond to the play as they read it. The questions correspond to specific lines in the play and are followed by answers or sample responses. You may want to use these questions and comments to aid students who are having difficulty with the play; they can provide an opportunity to stop and catch up on the plot or understand the thinking of a character.

Act I   Scene 1

? BEFORE LINE 1, STAGE DIRECTION. *We are on a crowded street in Rome. It is lined with statues near what is today known as the Palatine Hill (which is where the palaces, or* palatia, *were). A joyous, peaceful crowd is milling about. Two tribunes—military men—enter with the noisy mob of commoners. What tone does Flavius's first speech immediately bring to the play?*

ANSWER. Flavius's imperious speech brings a hostile tone to the play, foreshadowing conflicts to come.

? LINE 15. *It is important in this play to watch the moods of the crowd. Do you think these commoners are afraid of the military men, or are they acting comically and boldly?*

ANSWER. The men are bold and mocking.

? LINE 35. *What do you think Marullus is doing as he speaks?*

ANSWER. Marullus could be threatening, pushing, or striking the men.

? LINE 52. *How* should *this short line be spoken?*

ANSWER. This angry command should be issued with great force.

? LINE 55. *What is the key word in the last line of this speech? Why is Marullus angry with the mob?*

ANSWER. The key word is *ingratitude*. Marullus is angry with the people's fickleness.

? FOLLOWING LINE 60, STAGE DIRECTION. *Pay attention to the movements of the crowd. What mood has taken over these commoners as they leave the stage? Would you have them leave in a defiant mood, or are they ashamed?*

ANSWER. Because the men exit silently and quickly, defiance is an unlikely mood. The tribunes have made the men feel ashamed for forgetting Pompey.

? LINE 75. *What does Flavius fear about Caesar?*

ANSWER. Flavius fears that Caesar will use his popularity with the masses to increase his power and rule Rome as a tyrant.

Scene 2

? BEFORE LINE 1, STAGE DIRECTION. *As Caesar and his retinue enter, the crowd makes way for them. Antony is dressed for the race held on the feast of Lupercal, which this year also celebrates Caesar's latest victory. Caesar is most likely richly dressed—perhaps too richly. What mood would Marullus and Flavius be in?*

ANSWER. They would not be in a festive mood; more likely they would feel resentment over the celebration and scorn for the masses.

? LINE 10. *This speech suggests something important about Antony. What is it?*

ANSWER. Antony is loyal.

? LINE 13. *A lot of ceremonial music and ritual has opened this scene, so our attention has been focused on Caesar and his followers. But now the soothsayer, a teller of the future, is suddenly visible. This is a dramatic moment, for it foreshadows what will happen. Where would you place the soothsayer? How might Caesar react to his call?*

ANSWER. The soothsayer should be visible to the audience but not to Caesar. He should be positioned to step out and stand alone. Caesar might

*Drama Study Guide: **The Tragedy of Julius Caesar***

react with mixed emotions, both irritated and disturbed.

? LINE 17. *What physical disability does this line suggest?*

ANSWER. Caesar is deaf in one ear.

? LINE 18. *The ides of March is March 15. In some productions this warning is heard as an ominous and disembodied cry. In what different ways could the line be spoken?*

ANSWER. The line could be sinister, forceful and prophetic, fearful, or mysterious.

? FOLLOWING LINE 24, STAGE DIRECTION. *The stage is empty for a few moments as Brutus and Cassius stand looking at the departing Caesar. The plot line of the play—the assassination—begins now with Cassius's rather casual question. How should Brutus answer?*

ANSWER. Brutus's answer should show that he is preoccupied, perhaps deliberately separating himself from the celebrants.

? LINE 47. *How does Brutus explain his behavior?*

ANSWER. Brutus says that he has been troubled and has turned inward, trying to sort out conflicting emotions.

? LINE 60. *How should Cassius say the parenthetical remark?*

ANSWER. Cassius should speak sarcastically.

? LINE 78. *What, in sum, is Cassius telling Brutus here?*

ANSWER. Cassius is saying that he does not give friendship easily and can be trusted.

? FOLLOWING LINE 78, STAGE DIRECTION. *The trumpet sounds offstage, and the crowd's roar is heard again. How should Cassius and Brutus react?*

ANSWER. They should show alarm.

? LINE 80. *This is what Cassius has wanted to hear. How should he deliver this speech?*

ANSWER. Cassius should speak quickly, with energy and passion. He might also show his joy that Brutus agrees with him.

? LINE 89. *Brutus could sound noble here, or he could be played as foolishly idealistic, even priggish. How would you deliver this speech?*

ANSWER. Students may support either interpretation but should see that Brutus has so far shown himself to be thoughtful and not so foolishly idealistic that Cassius does not desire his aid.

? LINE 97. *This is a long and important speech. What is Cassius's chief complaint about Caesar?*

ANSWER. Cassius complains that Caesar has set himself up as a god.

? LINE 118. *How should Cassius say this sentence?*

ANSWER. Cassius should speak with bitterness, outrage, or sarcasm.

? LINE 121. *What word should be stressed here?*

ANSWER. Cassius should stress *god.*

? LINE 131. *Why has Cassius told these anecdotes about Caesar? What is his point?*

ANSWER. His stories show that Caesar is unworthy to rule Rome, a mere mortal who has no right to proclaim himself a god. He wants to persuade Brutus to join the conspiracy.

? LINE 142. *There is often a pause here, after the Colossus metaphor. How should Cassius say the names* Brutus *and* Caesar?

ANSWER. Cassius should articulate these names because he is presenting them for consideration and comparison. He could give them equal weight or show a preference for one or the other.

? LINE 161. *Why does Cassius mention Brutus's famous ancestor?*

ANSWER. Cassius is appealing to Brutus's sense of pride and honor.

? LINE 177. *According to Cassius's speech, how has Brutus delivered his previous line? Has Cassius gotten what he wants?*

ANSWER. Brutus has spoken with spirit and determination. Cassius has achieved a first step.

? FOLLOWING LINE 177, STAGE DIRECTION. *Cassius and Brutus move downstage left to allow the procession (Caesar's train) to pass across the width of the backstage area to an entrance down right. In this way the audience sees two acting areas at one time—one for the conspirators and their growing intimacy and one for the pompous world of public ceremony. Should the two actors next speak openly, or are they already acting secretively?*

Drama Study Guide: **The Tragedy of Julius Caesar**

ANSWER. They are already secretive, keenly observing Caesar and his followers.

? LINE 188. *Cicero at this time is sixty-two years old, famous as a great advocate of the republic. Though he had supported Pompey and opposed Caesar, Cicero likes Caesar personally and will have nothing to do with the assassination. What does Brutus think of Cicero?*

ANSWER. Brutus characterizes Cicero as a sly person (a weasel) who reacts violently when crossed.

? LINE 190. *Cassius and Brutus move away, and we focus on Caesar, who casts a suspicious look at Cassius, now downstage left. What does Caesar's next speech tell us about Cassius's physical appearance?*

ANSWER. Cassius is a thin and intense man, perhaps with a furtive manner.

? LINE 212. *Caesar's analysis of Cassius is accurate. Why does he fear Cassius? What does the speech tell us about Caesar himself?*

ANSWER. Caesar fears Cassius's insightfulness and his hunger for power, which he believes is fueled by envy. Caesar himself is too vain to admit to fear and tries to assume the heroic public self that he has created.

? FOLLOWING LINE 214, STAGE DIRECTION. *As the procession leaves through an upstage portal at left, Brutus pulls on Casca's toga as he passes. Casca is rough and sarcastic. How is his sarcasm suggested in the following lines?*

ANSWER. Casca shows sarcasm by not answering questions directly and using particular descriptions, such as *gentler* and *honest* (lines 229–230).

? LINE 232. *How does Brutus respond to this news about the crown?*

ANSWER. Brutus is seriously concerned and apprehensive.

? LINE 248. *How does Casca feel about the Roman mob?*

ANSWER. Casca finds them repulsive and laughable.

? LINE 254. *What do you think Cassius means here?*

ANSWER. Cassius could be punning on several meanings of *fall* and *falling* to justify the conspiracy. A fall is a defeat or a collapse, and the phrase *falling-sickness* also suggests the subservience that Caesar could impose.

? LINE 273. *Casca gets very sarcastic here. What does he think of Caesar?*

ANSWER. Casca believes that Caesar is an insincere showman courting the favor of the crowd and secretly desiring to be king. Casca also acknowledges Caesar's power over these impressionable people.

? LINE 285. *Why are Marullus and Flavius silenced? What does this tell you about Caesar?*

ANSWER. They are silenced for removing from Caesar's statues decorations celebrating his triumphs. Caesar acts swiftly and harshly against those who oppose him.

? LINE 306. *Why do you think Cassius earlier uses the respectful* you *when talking to Brutus but switches to the familiar* thou *here?*

ANSWER. When he speaks directly to Brutus, he is respectful because he intends to manipulate. His switch to *thou* seems to reflect a mixture of contempt and regret that Brutus can be seduced.

? LINE 320. *What is Cassius going to write in the letters to Brutus? What does he hope these letters will accomplish?*

ANSWER. Cassius will write that Brutus is respected and will hint at Caesar's dangerous ambition. Cassius is using the letters to flatter Brutus and to try to convince him that the conspirators' cause is honorable.

Scene 3

? BEFORE LINE 1, STAGE DIRECTION. *In Shakespeare's day, other than a drum roll or "thunder sheet," there was no way to reproduce the drama of nature onstage. How can the actors themselves suggest the threatening weather?*

ANSWER. The actors can cower in reaction to thunder and lightning; they can shout to be heard over the storm; they can wear cloaks or hats and draw their clothing closely about them.

? LINE 13. *How is this depiction of Casca different from the earlier depiction?*

ANSWER. Casca now speaks without sarcasm. (Note that earlier he speaks in prose, and now he speaks in blank verse.)

? LINE 32. *Shakespeare often uses disorder in nature to suggest a nation's disorder. What does Casca think?*

Drama Study Guide: The Tragedy of Julius Caesar

34

HRW MATERIAL COPYRIGHTED UNDER NOTICE APPEARING EARLIER IN THIS WORK.

ANSWER. Casca believes that the events are a sign that the gods are angry and will visit destruction on Rome.

? LINE 35. *How does the aged Cicero respond to Casca's report?*

ANSWER. He agrees that the events are unusual but states that people often misinterpret natural occurrences.

? LINE 43. *Can you explain Cassius's response to the disordered night?*

ANSWER. Cassius interprets the events as a sign that Caesar is wicked and must be stopped. As an "honest" man, Cassius feels he is safe.

? LINE 72. *How might Cassius's tone of voice change here?*

ANSWER. Cassius might lower his voice to make a "dreadful" confidence.

? LINE 89. *Cassius would normally respond to this kind of news with anger. What is he holding in his hand?*

ANSWER. He is probably holding a dagger.

? LINE 100. *What is Cassius threatening to do?*

ANSWER. He is threatening to commit suicide.

? LINE 115. *Does Cassius mean that Casca is a willing slave of Caesar's? What reaction is he looking for?*

ANSWER. No, Cassius hopes Casca will angrily declare himself against Caesar.

? LINE 130. *Cassius has begun his conversation with Casca by showing him his dagger and threatening suicide as a way to free himself from bondage. At what point does the conversation shift to an altogether different method of freeing himself?*

ANSWER. Cassius gives hints of rebellious thoughts when he exclaims "But, O grief, / Where hast thou led me?" (lines 111–112). Cunningly he lets Casca first mention a faction "for redress of all these griefs" (line 118).

? LINE 139. *What is Cassius's mood?*

ANSWER. Cassius's impatience shows anxiety, perhaps about both his plans and the conspirators' loyalty.

? LINE 148. *What is Cassius asking Cinna to do?*

ANSWER. He is asking Cinna to put the anonymous letters where Brutus will discover them.

Act II   Scene 1

? BEFORE LINE 1, STAGE DIRECTION. *Brutus's garden often has a set of steps in the back, set in a half circle. Below the steps is a stone bench. On the right and left are the doorways of an impressive residence. The door to the left is the servants' entrance, where Brutus directs his call to Lucius. Why is Brutus anxious about the time?*

ANSWER. The new day will be the ides of March.

? LINE 10. *Whom is Brutus talking about in this soliloquy?*

ANSWER. He is talking about Caesar.

? LINE 34. *According to Brutus, who is like a serpent's egg, and why?*

ANSWER. Brutus compares Caesar to a serpent's egg; crowning him will unleash his evil nature, just as hatching sets free a "mischievous" snake.

? FOLLOWING LINE 38, STAGE DIRECTION. *Whose letter is this?*

ANSWER. This is the letter that Cassius wrote and had Cinna deliver.

? LINE 40. *Does Brutus know of the soothsayer's warning?*

ANSWER. Yes.

? LINE 58. *How might Brutus act as he reads this message? What is his tone of voice at the end?*

ANSWER. Brutus probably reads contemplatively but reacts passionately. At the end his voice is fervent.

? FOLLOWING LINE 85, STAGE DIRECTION. *Describe what the stage looks like right now. From what is said of the conspirators, how would you imagine they are dressed?*

ANSWER. The six conspirators, their faces hidden by hats and cloaks, are grouped opposite Brutus, with Cassius standing in front of his five accomplices.

? LINE 100. *How would you have the actors placed onstage as Brutus and Cassius huddle and the others talk?*

ANSWER. The actors who are speaking would likely stand downstage. Brutus and Cassius might sit upstage center.

? LINE 152. *Why do they decide not to ask Cicero to join them?*

ANSWER. Brutus says he will not follow a plan that someone else begins.

? LINE 153. *What kind of person does Casca seem to be?*

ANSWER. He seems to be someone easily swayed by others.

? LINE 170. *How do you think the actor playing Brutus should speak this sentence?*

ANSWER. Brutus should speak with anguish.

? LINE 180. *What does Brutus want the public, or history, to think of him?*

ANSWER. He wants people to think he acted out of a love of liberty, not malice.

? LINE 191. *What do Brutus, Cassius, and Trebonius think of Antony?*

ANSWER. Brutus thinks Antony is ineffective without Caesar; Cassius fears him and his devotion to Caesar; Trebonius believes he is a survivor, a man without deep feelings.

? LINE 211. *According to Decius, what sort of man is Caesar? (What do you think of people like Decius?)*

ANSWER. Decius says that Caesar delights in others' weaknesses, but he shares these faults and is easily manipulated. Some may see Decius as a manipulator; others may view him as pragmatic.

? LINE 221. *How would you use lighting here to suggest the time?*

ANSWER. The lights could be brought up gradually to suggest the dawning of a new day.

? LINE 256. *Where is Portia now standing?*

ANSWER. By the end of this line, Portia is probably standing close to Brutus.

? LINE 260. *Some directors have Portia come very close to Brutus, physically and emotion-*

ally, and have him break away here. What might Portia's reactions be?

ANSWER. Portia might show her concern by following Brutus and grasping his toga.

? LINE 270. *What clue tells us what Portia does here? Is she becoming calmer or more agitated?*

ANSWER. "Upon my knees" shows that Portia is kneeling. Portia is becoming more distressed.

? LINE 278. *What is Brutus doing here?*

ANSWER. He is helping Portia rise.

? LINE 301. *What does Portia suddenly do to prove her patience and faithfulness? How do you think Brutus should respond?*

ANSWER. She shows Brutus a self-inflicted wound. (Both Brutus and Portia are followers of Stoicism, a philosophy that includes the mastery of pain and emotion.) Brutus is greatly moved. He might embrace her or turn away, overcome by emotion.

? LINE 321. *What action might Ligarius make with this line?*

ANSWER. He might remove his scarf.

? FOLLOWING LINE 334, STAGE DIRECTION. *Thunder is a kind of actor in Shakespeare's plays. What mood does it evoke? Would you have this thunder sound alone, or would you have it serve as background noise for these speeches?*

ANSWER. Thunder portends weighty actions and signals disturbance. Sounding alone, it would be a dramatic coda to the action; as background noise it would heighten the urgency of these speeches.

Scene 2

? LINE 26. *Calphurnia can be played here as hysterical and overly emotional or as truly frightened for her husband. Which way do you think the part should be played?*

ANSWER. You might ask volunteers to read Calphurnia's speech in at least two different ways.

? LINE 31. *What does Calphurnia mean?*

ANSWER. She believes that the horrors are omens of Caesar's death.

*Drama Study Guide: **The Tragedy of Julius Caesar***

LINE 37. *How does Caesar feel about death? How does his tone change when he addresses the servant?*

ANSWER. Caesar maintains that he is one of the brave few who are unafraid of death because they know that death is inevitable. Caesar becomes more arrogant when the servant enters.

LINE 37. *The augurers were very important in ancient Rome. Their duty was to tell from certain signs whether some action was favored by the gods. Signs were read in the flights of birds, in thunder, in the way sacred chickens ate their food, and in the condition of the organs of sacrificial animals. What is Caesar's mood as he hears of the augury this morning?*

ANSWER. Caesar says he is unafraid but is disturbed and unsettled by the night and by Calphurnia's dream.

LINE 48. *Caesar could end this speech with pomposity, dignity, or even humor. How do you interpret his tone?*

ANSWER. Ask students to defend their interpretations and discuss how each interpretation would affect the rest of the scene.

LINE 54. *What is Calphurnia doing?*

ANSWER. She is kneeling.

LINE 56. *Here is a sudden change. Would a kiss between lines 54 and 55 explain it?*

ANSWER. Yes. However, Calphurnia's distress could have risen to such a pitch that Caesar is truly frightened for her.

LINE 65. *Is Caesar angry or gentle?*

ANSWER. His speech indicates that he is angry.

LINE 83. *Remember what Decius is here for. We should sense his hungry absorption of Caesar's dream. How should he explain the dream—is he confident, fawning, awed, nervous?*

ANSWER. Decius, accustomed to manipulating Caesar, is likely to be confident.

LINE 91. *There should be a pause here. Caesar's fate is about to be sealed. Does he seem relieved or amused?*

ANSWER. He is probably relieved.

LINE 101. *What reaction from Caesar is Decius seeking when he refers to "Caesar's wife"? How is Decius playing on Caesar's fears?*

ANSWER. Decius hopes Caesar will bridle at the suggestion that he is ruled by his wife's whims. Caesar does not want his superstitions revealed.

LINE 107. *Suddenly Caesar changes his mind. Decius has succeeded. How might Calphurnia react now? Do you think Caesar concedes because he foolishly believes Decius or because he heroically accepts his fate?*

ANSWER. Calphurnia might react to Decius with horror or anger; she might cower before Caesar. Use this question to discuss the conflicting impressions of Caesar conveyed in this scene.

FOLLOWING LINE 107, STAGE DIRECTION. *What mood would the conspirators be in as they approach their victim?*

ANSWER. The conspirators are no doubt resolute, but they may express some fear, nervousness, sorrow, or shame.

LINE 113. *Where else has Caesar mentioned that a character is lean?*

ANSWER. In Act I, Scene 2, line 194, Caesar says, "Yond Cassius has a lean and hungry look."

LINE 117. *How can the actors playing Antony and Caesar establish the deep friendship that exists between them?*

ANSWER. They can show delight in seeing each other; they can clasp hands; they can speak in familiar tones.

LINE 124. *Asides are addressed to the audience, out of hearing of the other actors. How might this aside be spoken?*

ANSWER. Trebonius probably speaks this aside maliciously.

LINE 127. *What irony do we feel here? (What do we know that Caesar is ignorant of?)*

ANSWER. We feel dramatic irony because we realize, but Caesar does not, that his friends are really his most dangerous enemies.

Scene 4

LINE 9. *In this speech, is there a clue that Brutus has told Portia of the conspiracy to murder Caesar? Does the script provide an opportunity for him to tell her after their conversation in Scene 1? In "stage time" (the times at which the play's events take place), could he have told Portia of the plot?*

Drama Study Guide: The Tragedy of Julius Caesar

HRW MATERIAL COPYRIGHTED UNDER NOTICE APPEARING EARLIER IN THIS WORK.

37

ANSWER. Yes, she is struggling not to reveal a secret. No, at the end of Scene 1, Brutus exits without speaking to Portia.

> **LINE 46.** *What is Portia's state of mind? Why might she deliver line 45 after a pause?*

ANSWER. Portia is torn between devotion to Brutus and horror at the murder. She might pause as she tries to devise a message Brutus will understand and Lucius will not.

Act III   Scene 1

> **BEFORE LINE 1, STAGE DIRECTION.** *This scene takes place on the Capitol Hill, where the temple of Jupiter is located. A half circle of steps is seen at the back of the stage, with a throne on top. To the side is seen a statue of Pompey—the enemy Caesar defeated in the recent civil war. Caesar walks to center stage, and the others flank him. How should Caesar regard the soothsayer and Artemidorus? Should he address his first remark to the soothsayer or to the crowd in general?*

ANSWER. Caesar should pay attention to them. He should address the soothsayer first.

> **LINE 8.** *Is this sincerity or false humility?*

ANSWER. Caesar is falsely humble.

> **LINE 10.** *Publius speaks to Artemidorus, and the conspirators rush the petitioner away from Caesar. Whom is Cassius addressing in the next speech?*

ANSWER. He is addressing the group following Caesar.

> **LINE 13.** *Popilius speaks to Cassius. Do you think he knows about the conspiracy?*

ANSWER. Popilius seems to know.

> **LINE 26.** *Why is Trebonius getting Antony out of the way?*

ANSWER. Antony might hinder the murder.

> **LINE 29.** *What is happening near Caesar now?*

ANSWER. The conspirators are arranging themselves around him, as planned.

> **LINE 48.** *What does Caesar do during this speech? What does Metellus do in response to Caesar's words?*

ANSWER. Caesar commands Metellus to rise. Metellus perhaps continues bowing and fawning, provoking Caesar to push him away.

> **LINE 51.** *Whom is Metellus addressing here?*

ANSWER. He is appealing to the senators.

LINE 52. *Brutus steps forward; notice that he uses the pronoun* thy *in an insulting way, since Caesar is neither his social inferior nor an intimate. How might Caesar react to Brutus's surprising words?*

ANSWER. Caesar might be outraged or merely taken aback.

> **LINE 70.** *At what point in this speech would Caesar rise from his throne? The senators now rush in around Caesar and, in most productions, kneel before him. Casca has worked his way in back of Caesar.*

ANSWER. Caesar would rise at "and that I am he" (line 70) or on the earlier words "but one" (line 68).

> **LINE 75.** *This line is often spoken to show Caesar's great fondness for Brutus. How else might it be spoken?*

ANSWER. An actor might emphasize Caesar's arrogance and anger.

> **LINE 76.** *What does this line mean? What does Casca do?*

ANSWER. Casca means that his actions speak for him. Casca is the first to stab Caesar.

> **LINE 77.** *The murder of Caesar has been staged in many ways. Low-budget productions have to worry about laundry bills for cleaning stained togas, but most productions show blood. In some productions each dagger has attached to it a plastic capsule, which the actors break with their fingernails. In other productions, Caesar has a "blood" bag concealed under his toga. To stage the murder, directors often have the conspirators standing at different places onstage— all points to which Caesar runs in his attempt to escape. The last spot is Brutus's place. What does*

*Drama Study Guide: **The Tragedy of Julius Caesar***

Caesar see as he utters his last words? Why does he say, "Then fall Caesar"?

ANSWER. He sees that Brutus is one of the assassins. One interpretation of Caesar's words is "If this friend wants to kill me, I do not want to live."

? **LINE 107.** *What are the conspirators doing now?*

ANSWER. They are staining their hands and swords with Caesar's blood.

? **LINE 118.** *These speeches can be delivered in various ways. Would you emphasize the self-righteousness of the conspirators or their idealism?*

ANSWER. As students discuss this question, ask them how each delivery—sincere idealism or exaggerated fervor—would affect the dramatic conflict to follow between Brutus's faction and those loyal to Caesar.

? **LINE 137.** *What does Antony ask of Brutus?*

ANSWER. Antony asks Brutus to promise he will be safe if he comes to the Capitol.

? **LINE 146.** *How does Cassius say this line? Notice that at this moment the play takes a turn and that the hunters now become the hunted.*

ANSWER. Cassius is worried and on his guard.

? **LINE 151.** *Where should Antony position himself? In this speech, where would you have the actor playing Antony pause? What movements or gestures might he make?*

ANSWER. Antony should be near Caesar's body. A natural break occurs at the end of line 150. Antony might stoop to Caesar's body and then rise to face the conspirators. He might draw attention to their bloody swords and gesture pleadingly.

? **LINE 178.** *What differences in character do Brutus and Cassius reveal here in replying to Antony?*

ANSWER. Brutus, an idealistic man of feeling, assures Antony that the conspirators have "pitiful" hearts and welcome him as a brother. Cassius, a practical man of politics, assures Antony that the conspirators will share power with him.

? **LINE 185.** *This is a rather bold step on Antony's part. What is he doing?*

ANSWER. Antony shakes hands with each man.

? **LINE 194.** *What is Antony's position onstage now—is he standing or kneeling? Is he near the corpse or far away from it?*

ANSWER. Antony is near the corpse; he might be standing or kneeling.

? **LINE 210.** *Why is the imagery of the hunted deer ("hart") so appropriate here? How does it make you feel about Caesar?*

ANSWER. Like a lone deer trapped by organized hunters, Caesar was defenseless and unsuspecting. Antony's imagery arouses pity and imbues Caesar with natural majesty.

? **LINE 254.** *How should Antony's tone now change? Whom is he talking to?*

ANSWER. Antony's tone should show grief and rage. He is speaking to Caesar.

? **LINE 263.** *During this speech some directors let us hear the offstage noise of the crowd. At what moments in this speech would the offstage cries of the mob and even other street noises be appropriate?*

ANSWER. The noise could begin at line 260 and continue through the speech, or it could punctuate lines 260–261, 265–268, and 272–275.

? **LINE 284.** *What might Antony do to the servant to make us feel his compassion?*

ANSWER. He might touch his shoulder or gently move him away from the body.

? **LINE 297.** *Would you end this scene with Antony raising the body in his arms, or would you have him stand over it? Would the noise of the crowd be heard from offstage?*

ANSWER. As students give their responses, ask them to describe what would be conveyed if Antony stood alone at Caesar's feet or if he lifted the body, embracing it. Crowd noises would heighten Antony's plotting and prepare for the mob scene in the Forum.

Scene 2

? **BEFORE LINE 1, STAGE DIRECTION.** *The Roman Forum was a busy, crowded, open area. At one end of the Forum was the rostrum, a pulpit from which Rome's great public figures spoke. In stage sets the pulpit is usually set on a semicircular platform with steps leading up to it. This scene is wild and noisy. What is Brutus's mood as he fights free of the mob and goes up to the pulpit?*

ANSWER. Brutus is impatient to confront and appease the people.

Drama Study Guide: The Tragedy of Julius Caesar

HRW MATERIAL COPYRIGHTED UNDER NOTICE APPEARING EARLIER IN THIS WORK.

39

LINE 35. *Notice that Brutus's speech is in prose, not poetry. What value does Brutus presume the people cherish—as he cherishes it?*

ANSWER. Brutus believes they cherish reason and plain speaking instead of emotional appeal.

LINE 52. *Why is this cry from the mob, in lines 52–53, ironic? Has the crowd understood Brutus's motives at all?*

ANSWER. They want Brutus to assume the power from which he tried to save them. No, they offer statues and crowns—symbols of the despotism Brutus wanted to destroy.

LINE 54. *What should Antony be doing while the mob is talking? (Remember, he has brought Caesar's body to the Forum.)*

ANSWER. Antony should be standing respectfully near the body, but he should be watching closely, sizing up the crowd.

LINE 75. *An important question: Where would you place Caesar's body so that Antony can use it most effectively? Be sure to perform this famous funeral oration. What tones do you hear in it?*

ANSWER. By moving the body to the pulpit, Antony can keep it in the people's view as he speaks. The body might also be isolated to create the effect of a character surrounded by death. Ironic or sympathetic tones may be heard in the oration.

LINE 100. *Remember that the crowd is pressing in on Antony. What movements or sounds would they make as Antony says things that are meant to sway their feelings?*

ANSWER. Persons in the crowd might repeat his phrases, make gestures to show their agreement, and draw their neighbors' attention to certain points.

LINE 109. *What do lines 108–109 mean? What could Antony do at this point, as our attention is drawn again to the crowd?*

ANSWER. Antony has been overcome by his grief and must recover his composure. He could weep, turn his back, or lean against the coffin to contemplate Caesar.

LINE 139. *Antony says he is not going to read the will. But what has he already implied about its contents?*

ANSWER. He has implied that the people are its beneficiaries.

LINE 148. *Again, how has Antony scored his point indirectly? How might an actor play Antony in this scene to make him seem manipulative?*

ANSWER. Antony primes the mob to react with anger to Caesar's bequest. An actor might show Antony's manipulativeness by overacting. He might make his pauses lengthy so the mob will beg him to continue.

LINE 154. *The irony here is so obvious that an actor playing Antony must make a choice about how to say these lines: Will he continue his pretense of honoring Caesar's assassins, or will he finally drop this pose and speak with obviously scathing sarcasm?*

ANSWER. Have students consider how the choice affects the remainder of the speech and the audience's perception of Antony for the rest of the play.

LINE 169. *How do you visualize the placement of the actors at this point? Where is Caesar's body?*

ANSWER. The actors are ringed about Antony and the corpse. As a focal point in the scene, Caesar's body is now center stage.

LINE 172. *Watch for clues that tell what Antony is doing for effect as he delivers this speech. What is he holding in line 172?*

ANSWER. Antony is holding Caesar's cloak or toga.

LINE 195. *What is the crowd doing as Antony speaks?*

ANSWER. The people are crying.

LINE 198. *What has Antony done with the body now?*

ANSWER. Antony has fully revealed the body.

LINE 216. *Notice that Antony implies that reasons have not already been given. Have they?*

ANSWER. Brutus has given his reasons, but Antony implies that the conspirators have "private griefs" not yet divulged.

LINE 224. *How does Antony characterize himself, as compared with Brutus? What is his motive?*

ANSWER. Antony characterizes himself as a plain speaker, Brutus as an orator. Because Antony's motive is in fact "to stir men's blood," he wants the crowd to believe that Brutus is devious and self-interested.

*Drama Study Guide: **The Tragedy of Julius Caesar***

LINE 231. *Again, the irony is obvious here. What is the key word in this speech?*

ANSWER. The key word is *mutiny*.

LINE 240. *Notice how many times the mob goes to run off and Antony pulls it back again. How do you think Antony feels about this herd of people he has so cleverly manipulated?*

ANSWER. Antony sees them as gullible and as a tool for his ends, but students may also think that he shares some of Caesar's feeling for the populace.

LINE 263. *Antony is alone onstage. The noise of the mob dies off in the distance. We might in some productions see the reflection of flames* and hear the sounds of rioting. How should Antony speak these lines?

ANSWER. He should sound triumphant and ready for whatever comes.

LINE 271. *What have Brutus and Cassius done?*

ANSWER. Brutus and Cassius have fled the city.

Scene 3

LINE 39. *What has the mob done to the innocent poet Cinna?*

ANSWER. They have killed Cinna. Although Shakespeare does not specifically indicate the murder, Plutarch reports it.

Act IV   Scene 1

LINE 17. *What details suggest that this triumvirate is showing signs of strain? How has Antony changed from the person we saw in Act III?*

ANSWER. Antony and Lepidus tensely bargain over the death sentences of their relatives, and Antony insults Lepidus behind his back. Antony shows himself to be power-hungry, greedy, and disloyal.

LINE 27. *Who is compared to an ass?*

ANSWER. Lepidus is compared to an ass.

Scene 2

BEFORE LINE 1, STAGE DIRECTION. *Several months have passed since the assassination. Brutus and Cassius are in Sardis, the capital of ancient Lydia, a kingdom in Asia Minor. Why did Brutus and Cassius flee from Rome with their armies?*

ANSWER. Antony turned the Roman masses against the assassins; they fled for their lives.

LINE 18. *What details show that a split might be taking place in the conspirators' ranks?*

ANSWER. Brutus is displeased with something Cassius has done, and Cassius is only distantly courteous to Lucilius.

LINE 36. *What do you picture happening onstage here?*

ANSWER. As Brutus and Cassius meet, the soldiers pass along the line the order to halt.

Scene 3

LINE 12. *What has Brutus accused Cassius of?*

ANSWER. He has accused Cassius of taking bribes.

LINE 36. *What threat is Cassius making to Brutus?*

ANSWER. Cassius is prepared to fight.

LINE 57. *What did Cassius say?*

ANSWER. Cassius said he was "older in practice" and "abler" than Brutus to make military decisions (lines 31–32).

LINE 75. *What do you think of Brutus's moral position here? Does it seem honorable or hypocritical?*

ANSWER. Students will probably not think Brutus hypocritical. It is more likely that Brutus thinks unclearly; he does not see the inconsistency in refusing to raise money by "vile means" but being willing to spend money so raised.

LINE 99. *What does Cassius do, and why?*

Drama Study Guide: The Tragedy of Julius Caesar

HRW MATERIAL COPYRIGHTED UNDER NOTICE APPEARING EARLIER IN THIS WORK.

41

ANSWER. Cassius, to prove his love for Brutus, but also to shame him, tells Brutus to kill him.

LINE 102. *Notice that Cassius switches from* you *to* thou *here. Why?*

ANSWER. Cassius, in his anger, is trying to shame Brutus.

LINE 112. *Have Brutus's feelings changed? Why or why not?*

ANSWER. Brutus's fondness for Cassius has won out. He is no longer angry, even if he cannot condone Cassius's actions.

LINE 117. *What actions could mark the change in feelings now?*

ANSWER. Brutus and Cassius could embrace.

LINE 122. *How could a humorous note be sounded here?*

ANSWER. Brutus could act out the chiding by shaking his finger at Cassius.

LINE 134. *Remember that Shakespeare himself was a "jigging fool." What is the point of this scene with the poet?*

ANSWER. It is as if the author had walked into the play, a joke sure to amuse the audience. The scene also points out a contrast between Brutus and Cassius.

LINE 142. *This reference is to Brutus's philosophy of Stoicism, which taught that we should master our emotions, lead lives dictated by reason and duty, and submit to fate. How should Brutus deliver his next, shocking line?*

ANSWER. Brutus must speak impassively.

LINES 154–159. *Who is probably more emotional in this scene—Brutus or Cassius? (Many fine actors have shown no emotion as they played Brutus in this scene.)*

ANSWER. Cassius is more emotional.

LINE 178. *A peculiar scene now takes place, in which Brutus seems again to hear for the first time the news of his wife's death. Some scholars believe that the original account of Portia's death was told in lines 178–192 and Shakespeare later rewrote the scene, which is now lines 140–154. A production might not use both scenes. Which would you use, and why? (If both scenes are used, how should Brutus act in the second one?)*

ANSWER. The version in lines 140–154 is better because it connects Portia's death to Brutus's pre-vious behavior, shows more of Brutus's sorrow, and presents Cassius's grief more fully. The second version has an advantage in that it shows Brutus's reaction as he first learns of the death. If both scenes are used, Brutus should pretend ignorance (lines 179, 181) in order to avoid discussing his private sorrow.

LINE 189. *The actor playing Brutus must be careful not to make the character seem cold and unfeeling. How might this scene be played to suggest Brutus's humanity, as well as his Stoicism?*

ANSWER. Brutus might be portrayed as struggling to control his feelings.

LINE 199. *What plan does Cassius propose regarding Antony's forces at Philippi?*

ANSWER. Cassius wants to force Antony to march his troops to Sardis, a journey that will tire and weaken them.

LINE 221. *Where does Brutus want to fight Antony, and why?*

ANSWER. Brutus wants to fight at Philippi. He fears that if Antony marches on Sardis, men who are sympathetic to Antony's cause will join his forces along the way.

LINE 222. *Which man seems to dominate the action now?*

ANSWER. Cassius now yields to Brutus.

LINE 230. *In some productions at this point in the scene, Brutus takes a letter out of his pocket and burns it. What letter are we to assume he is destroying, and what does his action demonstrate?*

ANSWER. Brutus would be burning the letter that announced Portia's suicide. His action would show that he will put his grief behind him and move on.

FOLLOWING LINE 263, STAGE DIRECTION. *How could lighting be used to suggest an intimate, drowsy, and nonmilitary scene?*

ANSWER. The lights could fade and change to warmer colors. A director might use real candles or focus dim spotlights in certain places, leaving the rest of the stage dark.

LINE 278. *How would you stage the ghost? Would you have him in military dress? in his bloodied toga? Or would you not show the ghost at all, but merely project his voice onstage?*

ANSWER. Ask students to explain their reasons for their choices. What emotions would each choice evoke in the audience?

Drama Study Guide: The Tragedy of Julius Caesar

LINE 291. *In one production the ghost scene was staged so that the ghost's words seemed to come from the mouth of the sleeping Lucius. How would this explain Brutus's question to Lucius about "crying out"?*

ANSWER. Brutus would be much relieved if Lucius's dream explained the ghostly words.

Act V   Scene 1

BEFORE LINE 1, STAGE DIRECTION. *This act is crammed with action and can be confusing to follow. As you read, you might trace in your Reader's Log the movements of the armies. What props can be used to indicate that we are now on the plains of Philippi with Antony and Octavius's army?*

ANSWER. Flags, tents, and other equipment could indicate a military encampment.

FOLLOWING LINE 20, STAGE DIRECTION. *The armies should be placed at opposite sides of the stage, with a kind of no man's land between them. In the next lines, notice which man in which army speaks. The speakers are taunting one another across the short distance that separates them.*

ANSWER. Although all four issue taunts, Octavius and Brutus are more restrained than Antony and Cassius.

LINE 47. *What is Cassius referring to?*

ANSWER. Cassius wanted to kill Antony at the time of the assassination.

LINE 62. *Whom is Cassius taunting here? What does he think of this "new Caesar"?*

ANSWER. Cassius is taunting Octavius first and then Antony. Cassius thinks Octavius is whining, immature, and unequal to his title. Note also that Antony's comment about Cassius echoes Caesar's estimation of Cassius in Act I.

LINE 88. *What images in this speech suggest death and decay?*

ANSWER. Ravens, crows, and kites are carrion eaters; a canopy of shadows suggests the darkness of death; the expression *give up the ghost* means "to die."

LINE 92. *Remember that the two pairs of men have been talking separately. What action should now take place onstage?*

ANSWER. Brutus and Cassius come together for a final parting before each exits with his army.

LINE 107. *Brutus refers again to his Stoic philosophy, which taught that he should be ruled by reason, not by emotion. What is Brutus saying about suicide?*

ANSWER. He believes it cowardly to end one's life in order to avoid hardship.

LINE 109. *According to this speech, what will happen to the losing armies?*

ANSWER. The soldiers will be bound and paraded through the streets of Rome.

Scene 2

LINE 6. *What orders is Brutus giving his army?*

ANSWER. Brutus is ordering a sudden attack on Octavius's troops.

Scene 3

LINE 8. *What have Brutus's and Cassius's armies done?*

ANSWER. Cassius's men have run from the enemy. Brutus's men, flushed with success over Octavius's army, have begun looting.

LINE 24. *What is Cassius referring to here?*

ANSWER. Cassius is predicting that he will die that day, on his birthday.

LINE 26. *Pindarus stands on the upper stage, suggesting that he is on the hilltop, looking over the field of battle. What does he report to Cassius, who stands below?*

ANSWER. Pindarus reports that Titinius is surrounded by horsemen who overtake him, seize him as he dismounts, and shout for joy.

LINE 46. *What does Cassius have Pindarus do for him? What does Cassius believe has happened?*

---

*Drama Study Guide: **The Tragedy of Julius Caesar***

HRW MATERIAL COPYRIGHTED UNDER NOTICE APPEARING EARLIER IN THIS WORK.

43

ANSWER. Cassius has Pindarus kill him, using the sword with which Cassius killed Caesar. Cassius believes Titinius has been taken by the enemy.

? LINE 54. *Titinius and Messala enter from the wings and do not see Cassius's body at first. What irony do we in the audience feel when we hear their conversation?*

ANSWER. Titinius is free, not captured, as Cassius believed. The audience feels that Cassius has mistakenly sacrificed his life.

? LINE 65. *What does Titinius think caused Cassius to kill himself?*

ANSWER. Titinius thinks Cassius despaired of his success in carrying out the order.

? LINE 94. *Why does Brutus invoke Caesar's name?*

ANSWER. Brutus invokes Caesar's name because his assassination has led them to this battlefield. Brutus also seems to be remembering the ghost's message in Act IV, Scene 3, lines 279–280.

Scene 4

? LINE 7. *Lucilius is impersonating Brutus. What are these young men doing, and why?*

ANSWER. Their actions may be a diversionary tactic to protect Brutus and to divide Antony's troops.

? LINE 32. *Not long ago Antony was compiling a list of the enemies he was to have murdered. How does he seem to have changed?*

ANSWER. Antony seems more compassionate. He commands that a brave enemy be spared. However, his behavior is also a strategic change: "I had

rather have / Such men my friends than enemies" (lines 28–29).

Scene 5

? LINE 5. *What is Brutus's mood?*

ANSWER. Brutus's cynical remark shows his hopelessness.

? LINE 41. *What does he mean by saying that "night hangs upon" his eyes?*

ANSWER. Brutus means that his death is waiting for him.

? LINE 51. *How many bodies now lie on the stage? (It is important for a director of a Shakespearean tragedy to remember how many bodies are onstage. Getting rid of them is often a challenge.)*

ANSWER. There are four bodies—those of Cassius, Titinius, Cato, and Brutus.

? LINE 61. *How does Octavius indicate by his words to his former enemies that the strife is finally over?*

ANSWER. He offers to take Brutus's men into his service.

? LINE 81. *Order has been restored; healing will begin. What actor would you have exit last?*

ANSWER. Since Shakespeare makes Octavius the authority figure at the play's end, having Octavius exit last best supports the values embodied in the play. However, some students may prefer that Antony, a more compelling character, exit last.

Drama Study Guide: The Tragedy of Julius Caesar

Graphic Organizer for Active Reading, Act I

Who Is Caesar?

In Act I, we learn many things about Caesar, and most of what we learn comes from what other characters say about him. As you read Act I, use the chart below to study how Caesar is portrayed by other characters. In each character's oval, record the scene and line numbers of a passage spoken by that character about Caesar. Below each oval, summarize (briefly give the main idea of) that character's opinion of Caesar. Then, answer the questions that follow.

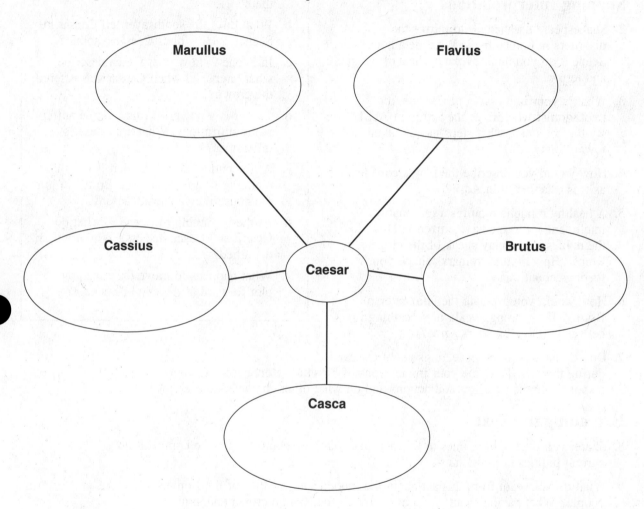

1. Choose one of the passages you selected above. What kind of imagery does the character use to portray Caesar? What effect do these images have on you?

   _____

   _____

2. Whose portrayal of Caesar do you find most believable? Why? _____

   _____

   _____

Making Meanings, Act I

First Thoughts

1. Can you think of any contemporary political leaders who are like Brutus and Cassius? Who are they?

Shaping Interpretations

2. Shakespeare uses nature to mirror the disorders in human lives. What details in Scene 3 do you think evoke a sense of danger and terror?

3. What is your impression of Cassius, the **protagonist** who drives the action in Act I? By the act's end, what steps has he taken toward his goal?

4. How would you describe the play's **conflict** as it is established in Act I?

5. A healthy republic requires a reasonably intelligent and responsive citizenry. How do the nobles in the play speak of the citizens of Rome? How do their remarks shape your feelings about them?

6. How would you evaluate the **character** of Brutus? Is he strong, weak, or something in between? (Do all readers agree?)

Reviewing the Text

a. Why are the workers celebrating in Scene 1? Why does Marullus yell at them?

b. What does the soothsayer tell Caesar in Scene 2? How does Caesar respond?

c. In Scene 2, how does Casca describe what happened when Caesar was offered the crown?

d. Caesar is a powerful ruler, yet he suffers many infirmities. What are Caesar's infirmities?

e. At the end of Scene 2, what is Cassius planning to do to persuade Brutus to join the conspiracy against Caesar?

f. At the beginning of Scene 3, what do Cicero and Casca discuss? Why are they disturbed?

g. What happens to move the conspiracy plot forward at the end of Scene 3?

---

7. Do you have conflicting feelings about Caesar during this act? Describe your impressions of his **character,** based on your responses to his speeches and actions and on what other characters say about him.

Extending the Text

8. Share with others some lines in this act that you think could be used to comment on current politics or politicians.

9. What do you learn from this act about the moods and loyalties of the Roman people? What parallels can you draw between the Roman crowd and similar gatherings today?

Drama Study Guide: The Tragedy of Julius Caesar

Choices: Building Your Portfolio, Act I

Performance

By Their Words You Will Know Them

Cassius and Brutus are clearly going to be important figures in the play. What kind of men are they? With a partner, choose a section of their dialogue, and prepare an oral reading of the conversation that reveals the character of each man. Present your dramatic reading to the class, and be sure to ask for feedback.

Vocabulary Mini-Lesson, Act I

Puns

Some people call puns juvenile humor, but Shakespeare's audiences enjoyed them. A **pun** is a word or phrase that means two different things at the same time. (Here's an old pun: What is black and white and read all over? Answer: a newspaper.)

In the first scene of *Julius Caesar,* when the cobbler says he is "a cobbler," he plays on two meanings of the word. (In Shakespeare's day, the word could mean either "shoemaker" or "bungler.") The cobbler also puns on the meaning of *soles. Soles* refers to parts of shoes but also sounds exactly like *souls.*

Some puns are based on two meanings of a word. Others involve **homophones,** words that sound alike but have different spellings and different meanings *(sole/soul).*

Here are two of Shakespeare's puns in Act I:

1. "... All that I live by is with the awl...." (Scene 1, line 21)

2. "I am ... a surgeon to old shoes: when they are in great danger, I recover them." (Scene 1, lines 23–24)

Try It Out

You could map the puns used by the cobbler and show the jokes like this:

Make maps that explain the puns in the two quoted lines shown on this page.

Use these words to make other pun maps:

lie	flour
son	break

Words to Own Worksheet, Act I

Developing Vocabulary

Carefully read each word's definition, explanation, and sample sentence. The definition and the sample sentence are based on the meaning of the word as it is used in *Julius Caesar*. Many of these definitions are now archaic. Write a sentence of your own using the word.

1. **conspirators** (kən·spir′ət·ərz) *n. pl.* persons who secretly plot to carry out an evil or illegal act. ▲ This word is derived from a Latin word meaning "to breathe together."

   ■ People still debate whether Lee Harvey Oswald acted alone in assassinating John F. Kennedy or whether he was one of a group of conspirators. (list of characters)

   Original sentence: _____

   _____

2. **soothsayer** (sooth′sā′ər) *n.* fortuneteller. ▲ The Middle English word *sothseyere* means "a person who speaks the truth."

   ■ The old woman was respected as a soothsayer, and all the villagers relied on her predictions. (list of characters)

   Original sentence: _____

   _____

3. **exalted** (eg·zôlt′id) *adj.* glorified; praised. ▲ This word is from the Latin word *exaltus,* meaning "high."

   ■ After winning the world championship, the exalted athletes were given new cars. (Scene 1, line 60)

   Original sentence: _____

   _____

4. **servile** (sur′vəl) *adj.* submissive; like a slave. ▲ This word and other familiar words like *serve* and *servant* derive from the Latin word for slave.

   ■ Stanley's servile manner is annoying; I would rather see him stand up for himself. (Scene 1, line 75)

   Original sentence: _____

   _____

5. **barren** (bar′ən) *adj.* unable to bear children. ▲ *Barren* can also refer to land that will not produce crops or lacks vegetation.

   ■ The woman thought she was barren, but then she happily discovered that she was going to have a baby. (Scene 2, line 8)

   Original sentence: _____

   _____

(*Continued on page 49.*)

*Drama Study Guide: **The Tragedy of Julius Caesar***

(Continued from page 48.)

ACT I

6. countenance (koun′tə·nəns) *n.* face.
▲ This word comes from a Latin word meaning "the way one holds oneself."

■ Russ was relieved to see his father's smiling countenance as he awoke from the operation. (Scene 2, line 38)

Original sentence: _____

_____

7. aught (ôt) *n.* anything. ▲ This archaic word is from the Old English word *awiht.*

■ Michael was confused by the question on the Shakespeare test, and he jokingly told his teacher, "The answer could be aught." (Scene 2, line 85)

Original sentence: _____

_____

8. torrent (tôr′ənt) *n.* a swift, violent stream.
▲ This word was borrowed from French in its present form.

■ The water came down the mountainside in a torrent. (Scene 2, line 107)

Original sentence: _____

_____

9. blunt (blunt) *adj.* abrupt; frank; outspoken.
▲ This word can also mean "dull; slow to understand."

■ Sometimes it is kinder to be blunt with someone than to hide the truth in order to protect his or feelings. (Scene 2, line 293)

Original sentence: _____

_____

10. portentous (pôr·ten′təs) *adj.* ominous; warning of things to come. ▲ Do not confuse *portentous* with *pretentious,* which means "flashy or showy."

■ The portentous swelling of the music signaled to the audience that another murder would soon occur. (Scene 3, line 31)

Original sentence: _____

_____

Drama Study Guide: The Tragedy of Julius Caesar

HRW MATERIAL COPYRIGHTED UNDER NOTICE APPEARING EARLIER IN THIS WORK.

49

Language Link Worksheet, Act I

Words Often Confused

MEG: If I say I'm coming to your party, is that an *acception*?

LI: No, silly, it's an *exception*.

MEG: You mean I'll be the only one to come?

Of course *acception* is not a word, but the conversation points to a common confusion: How do *accept* and *except* differ? Listed below are these two and other commonly confused words, as well as sample sentences based on characters in *The Tragedy of Julius Caesar*.

accept, except—*Accept* is a verb that means "to receive." *Except* as a verb means "to leave out." As a preposition, *except* means "excluding" or "other than."

> Caesar doesn't **accept** the crown.
> Antony is **excepted** from wearing a formal gown.
> Cassius seems to admire no man **except** Brutus.

advice, advise—*Advice* is a noun that means "a suggestion about what to do." *Advise* is a verb that means "to offer a suggestion, to recommend."

> Cassius's **advice** to Casca is welcome.
> "I **advise** you to look after your affairs" was his warning.

affect, effect—*Affect* is a verb that means "to influence." *Effect* as a verb means "to accomplish." As a noun, *effect* means "the result of an action."

> Cassius hopes to **affect** Brutus's attitude toward Caesar.
> Antony's speech **effected** exactly what he desired.
> The **effect** of Antony's speech was immediate.

allusion, illusion—An *allusion* is an indirect reference to something. An *illusion* is a mistaken idea or a misleading appearance.

> Cassius made an **allusion** to Caesar's secret illness.
> Is Caesar's reluctance to accept the crown an **illusion,** or is it real?

complement, compliment—As a noun, *complement* means "something that makes whole or completes"; as a verb, *complement* means "to make whole or complete." As a noun, *compliment* means "praise." As a verb, *compliment* means "to express praise."

> The crown would have been a **complement** to Caesar's ambition.
> Caesar's refusal of the crown **complemented** his humble nature.
> Antony delivered his sly words about Brutus as if they were a **compliment.**
> Antony said, "I would like to **compliment** Brutus on his honorable actions."

council, counsel—The noun *council* is "a group called together to accomplish a task." As a verb, *counsel* means "to advise." As a noun, it means "advice."

> The **council counseled** Caesar to conquer Phillipi. Caesar considered this **counsel** wise.

imply, infer—*Imply* means "to suggest indirectly." *Infer* means "to interpret" or "to draw a conclusion." We often *infer* from what is *implied*.

> Cassius didn't mean to **imply** that he hated Caesar.
> Some readers **infer** that Cassius is jealous of Caesar.

(Continued on page 51.)

*Drama Study Guide: **The Tragedy of Julius Caesar***

(Continued from page 50.)

principal, principle—As an adjective, *principal* means "main or most important." As a noun, *principal* means "the head of a school." *Principle* is a noun that means "a rule of conduct," "a belief," or "a general truth."

> This belief could be seen as his **principal** motivation.
> Our **principal** has arranged for a theater group to perform *Julius Caesar*.
> The **principle** on which Cassius bases his actions is that no man should be a slave.

EXERCISE A   Using the Correct Word

In each of the following sentences, which are based on details in *The Tragedy of Julius Caesar,* circle the word in parentheses that *best* completes the sentence.

1. Cinna argues that Brutus would (*complement, compliment*) their newly formed faction.

2. Brutus would (*accept, except*) Caesar as a ruler, (*accept, except*) he fears that Caesar will become a tyrant.

3. When Cassius speaks of the falling-sickness, it is an (*allusion, illusion*) to what the conspirators' future may be.

4. From what Cassius says, we can (*imply, infer*) that Casca is pretending to be slow-witted.

5. The storm (*affects, effects*) Casca and Cassius in different ways.

6. Caesar won't (*accept, except*) the soothsayer's (*council, counsel*).

7. Antony is Caesar's (*principal, principle*) admirer, and he is a youthful (*complement, compliment*) to Caesar's age and experience.

8. Marullus (*advices, advises*) the cobbler and the carpenter to stop celebrating.

9. Perhaps the soothsayer should (*advice, advise*) Cassius to stay out of the storm.

10. What (*council, counsel*) would you offer Caesar at the end of Act I?

EXERCISE B   Revising a Paragraph

The following paragraph contains errors in the use of some words. As you identify each error, cross out the incorrect word and write the correct word above it. As an example, the first error has been corrected for you. Find six more. The paragraph is based on details in *The Tragedy of Julius Caesar.*

Are Caesar's ambition and power ~~allusions~~? *(illusions)* In Act I, Cassius argues that Caesar is effected by his power and will inevitably become a tyrant. It is a complement to Shakespeare's skill as a writer to say that Cassius's principal motivation at the beginning of the play is not entirely obvious. Can we imply from Cassius's words that he is jealous of Caesar's growing power? Or should we accept Cassius's words at face value? Since the storm at the end of the act is an illusion to the storm that will soon erupt in the Roman state, we know that whatever Cassius's motives, the effects of his actions will not be peaceful. Cassius is skilled at complimenting others in order to persuade them to join his counsel. Soon, despite the advice of the soothsayer, Caesar will walk into the storm created by Cassius. Whatever we may infer from Cassius's motives, we must consider that he is concerned with the principal of freedom, whether it be for himself or for others.

Literary Elements Worksheet, Act I

Setting

Setting is the time and place of a play. It is established early in the story. Setting also includes the entire background of things and customs that go with a certain time and place. For example, you would expect the events of a presidential campaign to contribute to a play set in Washington, D.C., in 1996.

Understanding Setting

Match each setting clue with the best answer from the list below by writing the letter on the line at the left of the item. Some answers are used twice.

a. The time period is a pagan, not a Christian, era.

b. The horse is still the main means of transportation.

c. Workers get some days off.

d. The place is the city of Rome.

e. One scene occurs on a stormy night.

f. Some are discontented with the way things are going under Caesar, the current political leader.

_____ **1.** References are made to chariot wheels and chariots.

_____ **2.** Soothsayers are taken seriously.

_____ **3.** People are celebrating the Lupercal, a pagan fertility festival.

_____ **4.** Aeneas, legendary ancestor of the Roman people, is called "our great ancestor." (Scene 2, line 12)

_____ **5.** Working people are dressed in their best clothes.

_____ **6.** "What conquest brings he home? / What tributaries follow him to Rome. . . ?" (Scene 1, lines 32–33)

_____ **7.** "groaning underneath this age's yoke" (Scene 2, line 61)

_____ **8.** "I do fear the people / Choose Caesar for their king." (Scene 2, lines 79–80)

_____ **9.** "Good night then, Casca; this disturbèd sky / Is not to walk in." (Scene 3, lines 39–40)

Applying Skills

In "translating" the setting of a play to the stage, small, movable objects, called *props,* are used to help establish the setting. Imagine that you are the stage manager. Circle the words in these lines that alert you not to offstage objects but to props you must actually give to the actors.

1. "And do you now strew flowers in his way. . . ?" (Scene 1, line 50)

2. "You pulled me by the cloak; would you speak with me?" (Scene 2, line 215)

(Continued on page 53.)

Drama Study Guide: The Tragedy of Julius Caesar

(Continued from page 52.)

3. "I know where I will wear this dagger then. . . ." (Scene 3, line 89)

4. "Good Cinna, take this paper, / And look you lay it in the praetor's chair, / Where Brutus may but find it; and throw this / In at his window; set this up with wax / Upon old Brutus' statue." (Scene 3, lines 142–146)

Reader's Response

What feelings do you believe Shakespeare wanted to arouse in the viewer by establishing a stormy night as the setting for the conspirators' meeting? Circle those that seem appropriate.

awe	calmness	confusion	dread
foreboding	hint of evil	mystery	peace
secrecy	serenity	suspense	terror

Drama Study Guide: The Tragedy of Julius Caesar

Test, Act I

Thoughtful Reading (40 points)

On the line provided, write the letter of the *best* answer to each of the following items. *(8 points each)*

_____ 1. In Act I, the character who drives the action is

    a. Caesar   **c.** Brutus
    b. Cassius   **d.** Casca

_____ 2. Cassius's character can *best* be described as

    a. noble   **c.** cunning
    b. idealistic   **d.** honest

_____ 3. In Scene 3, Shakespeare uses a violent storm and other unusual natural events to suggest

    a. the onset of chaos in Rome
    b. the coming conflict between Cassius and Brutus
    c. Caesar's inner turmoil
    d. the coming intervention of the gods

_____ 4. The central conflict introduced in Act I is between

    a. Brutus and Cassius   **c.** Caesar and the soothsayer
    b. Brutus and Caesar   **d.** Caesar and his opponents

_____ 5. Caesar's observation that "yond Cassius has a lean and hungry look; / He thinks too much: such men are dangerous" is *not* an example of

    a. dramatic irony   **c.** figurative language
    b. foreshadowing   **d.** punning

Expanded Response (30 points)

6. Which word or phrase *best* describes that motivates the action in Act I? On the lines provided, write the letter of the answer you choose and briefly defend your choice. There is more than one possible answer. Use at least one example from the play to support your ideas. *(15 points)*

a. honor   **b.** tyranny   **c.** envy   **d.** flattery

_____

_____

_____

_____

_____

_____

_____

_____

_____

(Continued on page 55.)

Drama Study Guide: **The Tragedy of Julius Caesar**

(Continued from page 54.)

7. In the chart below, explain what events each of the following quotations from Act I may foreshadow (or hint will happen later in the play). *(15 points)*

Quote	What It Foreshadows
Brutus: "For let the gods so speed me, as I love / The name of honor more than I fear death." (Scene 2, lines 88–89)	
Cassius: "Men at some times are masters of their fates...." (Scene 2, line 139)	
Cassius: "'Brutus' will start a spirit as soon as 'Caesar.'" (Scene 2, line 147)	

Written Response *(30 points)*

8. In Scene 3, lines 34–35, Cicero says of the storm, "But men may construe things after their fashion, / Clean from the purpose of the things themselves." How does this differ from Cassius's attitude toward the storm? How else could the storm be interpreted? Write your answer on a separate sheet of paper, and use at least two examples from the play to support your ideas.

*Drama Study Guide: **The Tragedy of Julius Caesar***

Graphic Organizer for Active Reading, Act II

Who Is Brutus?

In Act II, we see Brutus take a leading role. Use the web below to construct a picture of Brutus's character. In each oval, write quotations and lines from the play that reveal what he is like. These may include Brutus's own words and actions, as well as the words and actions of others.

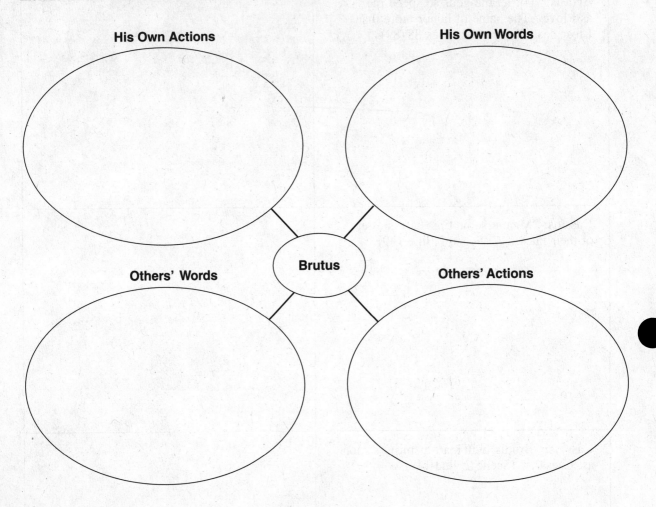

His Own Actions

His Own Words

Others' Words

Brutus

Others' Actions

1. What does Brutus's soliloquy at the opening of Act II reveal about his character?

_____

_____

_____

2. At this point in the play, whom do you consider the play's hero? Who is the villain? Why?

_____

_____

_____

*Drama Study Guide: **The Tragedy of Julius Caesar***

Making Meanings, Act II

First Thoughts

1. We all look for principles to tell us what's right and what's wrong. What principles have governed the choices Cassius and Brutus have made? Do you think their choices are wise? Are they "right"?

Shaping Interpretations

2. When you read rather than watch a play, you have to stage it in your imagination, to visualize the movements of characters and the sounds of voices. As you imagine Act II, tell how it compares with Act I—is the pace faster or slower? Are the characters more agitated or calmer? Which scenes make you think the way you do?

3. Why won't Brutus swear an oath (Scene 1, lines 114–140)? What **character traits** does this speech reveal?

4. Describe the complexities of Caesar's **character** that you've observed in this act. How do you feel about Caesar—is he a monstrous tyrant or a sympathetic man? Explain.

5. Where does Shakespeare use thunder and other storm sounds to suggest cosmic disorder? How does this weather make you feel?

Reviewing the Text

a. Look at Brutus's **soliloquy** at the beginning of Act II. What are the reasons he gives for killing Caesar?

b. Who proposes the murder of Antony? Why does Brutus oppose it?

c. What does Portia demand of her husband in Scene 1?

d. In Scene 2, what does Calphurnia try to persuade Caesar to do? Why?

e. How does Decius persuade Caesar to attend the Senate?

f. What is Portia's concern at the end of Scene 4?

Connecting with the Text

6. Describe how Shakespeare creates and builds **suspense** during Scenes 3 and 4.

7. Is Caesar's assassination necessary? Re-read Brutus's argument in Scene 1, lines 10–34—how would you respond to it?

Extending the Text

8. In Scene 4, Portia appears to know that Brutus is involved in a plot to kill Caesar, although the play does not include a scene in which Brutus gives her this information. Is this omission a weakness in the play? If you were writing such a scene, how would you have Portia react to her husband's news?

9. How do you feel about Portia's lament in her last speech in this act: "how weak a thing / The heart of woman is!"?

*Drama Study Guide: **The Tragedy of Julius Caesar***

ACT II

Choices: Building Your Portfolio, Act II

Performance

A Play Within a Play

Caesar's scene with Calphurnia and later with Decius (Scene 2) is a perfect play within a play.

Prepare the scene for performance. Before you begin to rehearse, be sure you understand what is driving the characters.

Vocabulary Mini-Lesson, Act II

Elizabethan English

The English language classifies words as nouns, verbs, and so on. When someone mixes up the parts of speech, purists are outraged. (Today, for example, purists deplore the use of the noun *network* as a verb.) Shakespeare freely used words as different parts of speech. Here he makes a verb out of the noun *conceit:*

> You have right well conceited.
> —Act I, Scene 3, line 162

Here he uses an adjective (*vulgar*) as a noun (we'd say "vulgar people"):

> And drive away the vulgar
> from the streets....
> —Act I, Scene 1, line 70

In some passages he omits words:

> ... So Caesar may;
> Then lest he may, prevent.
> —Act II, Scene 1, lines 27–28

What's understood here is "prevent him from doing it."

Try It Out

Use the footnotes in Act II for help with these questions.

1. In Scene 1, line 3, Brutus says he cannot "give guess how near to day." How would you expand this phrase?

2. What word does Brutus omit after the word *general* in line 12 of Scene 1?

3. What do you think Lucius means in Scene 1, line 73, when he says the conspirators' "hats are plucked about their ears"?

4. In Scene 1, line 83, what noun does Shakespeare use as a verb?

Drama Study Guide: **The Tragedy of Julius Caesar**

Words to Own Worksheet, Act II

Developing Vocabulary

Carefully read each word's definition, explanation, and sample sentence. The definition and the sample sentence are based on the meaning of the word as it is used in *Julius Caesar*. Many of these definitions are now archaic. Write a sentence of your own using the word.

1. **taper** (tā′pər) *n.* candle. ▲ The verb *taper* means "to gradually decrease in width or thickness."

   ■ Each pewter candlestick held a slender white taper. (Scene 1, line 7)

   Original sentence: _____

   _____

2. **spurn** (spurn) *v.* to reject or scorn. ▲ This word and *spur* (a device worn on the heel to urge a horse forward) come from the same language ancestor.

   ■ Rose spurned all Russell's offers of help. (Scene 1, line 11)

   Original sentence: _____

   _____

3. **base** (bās) *adj.* low in rank or position. ▲ *Base* still signifies "comparatively low worth" (copper is *base* metal; silver, a valuable one).

   ■ "Who is this base person?" asked the king, gesturing toward the peasant. (Scene 1, line 26)

   Original sentence: _____

   _____

4. **augmented** (ôg·ment′id) *adj.* made greater; enlarged. ▲ *Augment* comes from the Latin word *augere*, meaning "to increase."

   ■ The bait we bought at the tackle shop today, augmented by what we brought with us, should be enough to last us the week. (Scene 1, line 30)

   Original sentence: _____

   _____

5. **redress** (ri·dres′) *v.* to make compensation for. ▲ This word implies doing something in order to make up for a wrongdoing.

   ■ The young man was required to devote five hundred hours to community service to redress his crime. (Scene 1, line 47)

   Original sentence: _____

   _____

(Continued on page 60.)

Drama Study Guide: The Tragedy of Julius Caesar

(Continued from page 59.)

6. insurrection (in′sə·rek′shən) *n.* rebellion; uprising; revolt. ▲ This word and a related word, *insurgent* ("a person engaged in a revolt"), are derived from the prefix *in-,* which here serves as an intensifier, and the root *-surg-* ("to rise"). ■ Government troops were called in to put down the insurrection. (Scene 1, line 69)

Original sentence: _____

_____

7. visage (viz′ij) *n.* face. ▲ This word is based on the Latin word *visus,* meaning "a look." ■ The man peering through the window had a kindly visage, but I didn't recognize him. (Scene 1, line 81)

Original sentence: _____

_____

8. affability (af′ə·bil′ə·tē) *n.* friendliness; pleasantness. ▲ This word is based on the prefix *ad-,* which means "to," plus the Latin root *-fari-,* which means "to speak." You can remember the meaning of *affability* by thinking about a friendly person's willingness to speak to other people. ■ Marianne's affability causes other people to like her instantly. (Scene 1, line 82)

Original sentence: _____

_____

9. constancy (kän′stən·sē) *n.* faithfulness. ▲ This word is based on the prefix *com-,* which here means "together," and the Latin root *-stare-,* which means "to stand." ■ One of the qualities I most appreciate in a friend is constancy. (Scene 1, line 227)

Original sentence: _____

_____

10. imminent (im′ə·nənt) *adj.* likely to happen soon. ▲ Do not confuse this word with *eminent,* which means "famous or renowned." ■ Because landing was imminent, the flight attendant told us to fasten our seat belts. (Scene 2, line 81)

Original sentence: _____

_____

*Drama Study Guide: **The Tragedy of Julius Caesar***

Language Link Worksheet, Act II

Elizabethan English

Brutus.   Peace! count the clock.

Cassius.   The clock hath stricken three.
                            —Act II, Scene 1, line 192

When you read these lines, you know you are not reading words that you or your friends would use. To update Shakespeare's lines, you might write something like this:

Brutus.   Shh, listen to the chimes.

Cassius.   The clock has struck three.

Spoken language is a living thing; it changes with the times. New words are added; old words are dropped from our vocabulary. The uses and meanings of words also change, and even the way we order words in sentences shifts over time. When we read Shakespeare, we sometimes feel as if we need to translate his English into our English—and to a certain extent, we do. Consider these examples of how Shakespeare's English differs from our own.

Brutus.   ... O Rome, I make thee promise....
                    —Act II, Scene 1, line 56

Thee is not used in conversation today; instead of *thee,* we say *you*. We might say "I'll make you a promise" (adding the article *a* that is absent in Shakespeare's verse) or "I promise you."

Lucius.   Sir, March is wasted fifteen days.
                    —Act II, Scene 1, line 59

The verb *wasted* is used here simply to mean that the days have passed.

Lucius.   That by no means I may discover them
              By any mark of favor.
                    —Act II, Scene 1, lines 75–76

For us this would be a longer phrase—we might say "discover who they are."

Brutus.   And therefore think him as a serpent's egg....
                    —Act II, Scene 1, line 32

A word has been omitted here. We would say "think *of* him."

Brutus.   ... and to steel with valor
              The melting spirits....
          —Act II, Scene 1, lines 121–122

Here Shakespeare uses a noun, *steel,* as a verb.

EXERCISE   Understanding Shakespeare's Language

Answer each of the questions below by reading the specified lines in Act II and any footnotes that might apply. Sometimes it will help to read the text before and after the specified lines in order to gather meaning from context.

1. In Scene 1, line 51, what does the verb *piece* mean? _____

_____

2. In Scene 1, line 116, how is Shakespeare's word order different from what you would expect?

_____

_____

(Continued on page 62.)

Drama Study Guide: The Tragedy of Julius Caesar

(Continued from page 61.)

3. In Scene 1, line 117, what does the word *hence* mean? _____

_____

4. In Scene 1, line 141, what would you say instead of "sound him"? _____

_____

5. In Scene 1, line 154, what word would you use in place of *else,* and how would the word order of

that question be different today? _____

_____

6. In Scene 1, line 223, what words has Shakespeare left out? _____

_____

7. In Scene 1, line 235, what verb would replace *to commit* today? _____

_____

8. In Scene 1, line 276, what does Portia mean when she says "had resort to you"? _____

_____

9. How would you express Calphurnia's second question in Scene 2, line 8? _____

_____

10. What verb is left out in Scene 2, line 10? _____

11. What noun is used as a verb in Scene 2, line 27? _____

How would you say that line today? _____

_____

12. In Scene 2, line 75, what does *stays* mean? _____

How might the line be rewritten so that it sounds more modern? _____

_____

13. How would you say "have an eye to" as it is used in Scene 3, line 2?_____

_____

14. How do you interpret the meaning of the verb *press* in Scene 4, line 15? _____

_____

15. How would you translate into Modern English the question in Scene 4, line 23? _____

_____

*Drama Study Guide: **The Tragedy of Julius Caesar***

Literary Elements Worksheet, Act II

Characterization

Characterization is the process by which a writer reveals the personality of a character. Some methods of characterization in Shakespearean plays are (1) letting the audience hear the character speak, (2) revealing the character's private thoughts through speeches heard by the audience alone, and (3) showing how other characters react toward the character.

Understanding Characterization

After each detail characterizing Brutus, circle the letter of the *best* interpretation.

1. In a soliloquy—a speech to the audience that reveals a character's private thoughts—Brutus says,

   "It must be by his death; and for my part,
   I know no personal cause to spurn at him,
   But for the general. He would be crowned.
   How that might change his nature, there's the question." (Scene 1, lines 10–13)

   a. Brutus is eager to kill Caesar and take his place.

   b. Brutus has no strong personal dislike of Caesar.

2. Arriving with other conspirators, Cassius tells Brutus,

   ". . . no man here
   But honors you; and every one doth wish
   You had but that opinion of yourself
   Which every noble Roman bears of you." (Scene 1, lines 90–93)

   a. Brutus is highly respected in Rome.

   b. Brutus is held in low esteem in Rome.

3. Cassius proposes that the men swear an oath to kill Caesar, but Brutus says the word of a true Roman is enough (Scene 1, lines 114–140).

   a. Brutus is a man who believes in keeping his word.

   b. Brutus is afraid to have the gods witness the agreement.

4. Cassius argues that Mark Antony should also be killed, but Brutus argues against it (Scene 1, lines 162–183).

   a. Brutus is timid and fearful.

   b. Brutus will consider an execution but not a bloodbath.

(Continued on page 64.)

Drama Study Guide: The Tragedy of Julius Caesar

HRW MATERIAL COPYRIGHTED UNDER NOTICE APPEARING EARLIER IN THIS WORK.

63

(Continued from page 63.)

Applying Skills

Determine what each of the following details from the play tells you about Brutus. Write your interpretation on the lines provided.

1. Before the conspirators come, Brutus paces the floor during the night, saying,

"Since Cassius first did whet me against Caesar,
I have not slept.
Between the acting of a dreadful thing
And the first motion, all the interim is
Like a phantasma, or a hideous dream." (Scene 1, lines 61–65)

______

______

______

______

2. Ligarius is feeling sick, yet when Brutus asks him to join the plot against Caesar, Ligarius comes to attention and asks, "What's to do?"(Scene 1, line 326)

______

______

______

______

3. Portia is so worried about Brutus's pacing and lack of sleep that she sends a servant to keep an eye on him (Scene 4, lines 1–15).

______

______

______

______

Test, Act II

Thoughtful Reading (40 points)

On the line provided, write the letter of the *best* answer to each of the following items. *(8 points each)*

_____ 1. Brutus's soliloquy reveals his true feelings about

    a. Caesar   **c.** his servant
    b. Antony   **d.** his wife

_____ 2. Caesar's first decision not to go to the Senate is a response to

    a. the omens he perceives
    b. the words of Decius
    c. his desire not to appear ambitious
    d. the concerns of Calphurnia

_____ 3. Caesar alters his first decision to stay home when

    a. Calphurnia changes her mind and tells Caesar to go with Antony
    b. he consults the augurers, who tell him it is safe to go to the Senate
    c. Decius gives a positive interpretation of Calphurnia's dream
    d. Antony arrives to take Caesar to the Senate

_____ 4. Caesar disregards the omens for all of the following reasons except

    a. he does not trust the augurers
    b. he does not want to appear cowardly
    c. he feels that fate is inescapable
    d. he feels invincible

_____ 5. Brutus compares Caesar to a newly hatched serpent in order to show that Caesar is

    a. Rome's greatest leader
    b. corrupt and destructive
    c. capable of becoming a tyrant
    d. ineffective but honorable

Expanded Response (30 points)

6. Which word below *best* describes the roles of Portia and Calphurnia in relation to their husbands? On the lines provided, write the letter of the answer you choose, and briefly defend your choice. There is more than one possible answer. Use at least one example from the play to support your ideas. *(15 points)*

    a. submissive   **b.** devoted   **c.** self-sacrificing   **d.** selfish

_____

_____

_____

_____

_____

(Continued on page 66.)

Drama Study Guide: The Tragedy of Julius Caesar

ACT II

(Continued from page 65.)

7. Act II raises several suspenseful questions about what will happen to Caesar, to the conspirators, and to Rome. In the following chart, write three questions that are raised in the act. Beside each, write how the question is answered, or if it is not, make a prediction about how it will be answered later in the play. When you make a prediction, give a reason for your choice. A sample is done for you. *(15 points)*

Question	Answer or Prediction
Will Brutus join the conspiracy?	Yes, he joins it and takes on the role of leader.
1.	
2.	
3.	

Written Response *(30 points)*

8. In Scene 1, lines 63–69, Brutus says:

> "Between the acting of a dreadful thing
> And the first motion, all the interim is
> Like a phantasma, or a hideous dream.
> The genius and the mortal instruments
> Are then in council, and the state of a man,
> Like to a little kingdom, suffers then
> The nature of an insurrection."

How do these lines reflect both Brutus's inner conflict and the outer conflict that builds in Act II? Write your answer on a separate sheet of paper, and use at least two specific examples from the play to support your ideas.

*Drama Study Guide: **The Tragedy of Julius Caesar***

Graphic Organizer for Active Reading, Act III

Who Is Mark Antony?

Mark Antony has only a minor role in the play until Act III, when he becomes the major force moving the action. On the busts below, record lines from the play that contrast how Mark Antony is presented before Act III with how he is revealed in Act III. Then, on the lines provided below the busts, summarize your own view of Antony's character. You might consider these lines from Acts I and II; Act I, Scene 2, lines 9–10, 28–29, and 234–235; Act II, Scene 1, lines 155–184, and Scene 2, lines 52–53.

Before Act III   **In Act III**

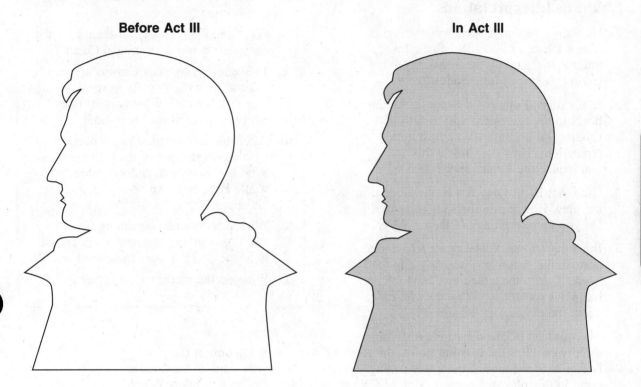

ACT III

The Real Antony: _____

_____

1. Do you consider Antony a hero or a villain or something in between? Explain.

_____

_____

_____

2. Make a prediction: What will happen as a result of Antony's having turned the crowd against the conspirators?

_____

_____

_____

*Drama Study Guide: **The Tragedy of Julius Caesar***

Making Meanings, Act III

First Thoughts

1. Brutus and Antony are both persuasive speakers. Whose funeral speech comes closer to expressing your own thoughts about Caesar's death? Why?

Shaping Interpretations

2. How does Antony's speech at the end of Scene 1 (lines 254–275) indicate his intentions regarding the assassins? What could this speech **foreshadow**?

3. In his funeral oration in Scene 2, Antony holds to his agreement with Brutus and Cassius yet destroys the conspirators' reputations. How does he do this and manipulate the Roman mob?

4. Until Act III, Antony has barely figured in the play. How have others characterized him? Do you agree with any of them? Why?

5. In earlier scenes, Shakespeare *tells* about lions in the streets and people going mad. In Scene 3, with the attack on Cinna the poet, he *shows* something. What does he reveal about the psychology of a mob?

Reviewing the Text

a. In Scene 1, a chance still exists that the conspiracy might be foiled. Why does Artemidorus fail to get Caesar to read his warning?

b. What petition serves as an excuse for the conspirators to gather around Caesar?

c. In Scene 1, why does Cassius argue against allowing Antony to speak at Caesar's funeral? What reasons does Brutus give for overruling him?

d. After the assassination the **protagonist** who drives the rest of the play appears. Who is this person, and what does he want? How have we been prepared for his appearance?

e. What information concerning Caesar's will does Antony disclose to the crowd in Scene 2? How does the crowd react?

f. What do the plebeians do in Scene 3?

6. The third act of Shakespeare's tragedies usually contains the **turning point,** the moment when all the action of the play begins to spiral toward the tragic ending. Which event do you think is the turning point in this play: the assassination of Caesar or Brutus's decision to allow Antony to address the crowd?

7. Lines 111–118 of Scene 1 seem to suggest that this play will be staged "many ages hence." What other interpretations of this passage do you think are possible?

Connecting with the Text

8. How do you feel about Brutus and Antony in this act? Do you see people like Antony and Brutus today? Explain.

Choices: Building Your Portfolio, Act III

Creative Writing

Behind the Scenes

Shakespeare never lets us see again the shoemaker from Act I. Suppose that shoemaker is in the crowd that listens to Brutus and Antony, carries away Caesar's body, and then kills the poet Cinna. Write a new scene in which the shoemaker and another character talk about what has happened on the ides of March. Perform your scene.

Drama Study Guide: The Tragedy of Julius Caesar

68

HRW MATERIAL COPYRIGHTED UNDER NOTICE APPEARING EARLIER IN THIS WORK.

Words to Own Worksheet, Act III

Developing Vocabulary

Carefully read each word's definition, explanation, and sample sentence. The definition and the sample sentence are based on the meaning of the word as it is used in *Julius Caesar*. Many of these definitions are now archaic. Write a sentence of your own using that word.

1. **firmament** (furm′ə·mənt) *n.* sky; heavens. ▲ This word comes from a Latin word meaning "a strengthening support."

   ■ Juan's poem began, "Alone in the <u>firmament</u> / a star twinkles for me." (Scene 1, line 62)

   Original sentence: _____

   _____

2. **valiant** (val′yənt) *adj.* brave; courageous. ▲ *Valiant* is derived from the Latin word *valere,* meaning "to be strong."

   ■ In Shauna's daydreams she always fought alongside <u>valiant</u> knights. (Scene 1, line 138)

   Original sentence: _____

   _____

3. **fetch** (fech) *v.* to get; to bring; to elicit. ▲ This word comes from the German word *fessen,* meaning "to grasp."

   ■ I taught my dog to <u>fetch</u> a stick. (Scene 1, line 142)

   Original sentence: _____

   _____

4. **beseech** (bē·sēch′) *v.* to beg. ▲ *Beseech* and *beg* are synonyms, but *beseech* implies anxiety over the outcome.

   ■ The woman dropped to her knees to <u>beseech</u> the king to spare her husband's life. (Scene 1, line 157)

   Original sentence: _____

   _____

5. **plebeians** (plē·bē′ənz) *n. pl.* common people. ▲ In ancient Rome the plebeians were the lower class and the patricians were the upper class.

   ■ When food supplies were short, the <u>plebeians</u> would often assemble in the square and <u>demand</u> that the wealthier citizens provide them with assistance. (Scene 2)

   Original sentence: _____

   _____

(Continued on page 70.)

Drama Study Guide: The Tragedy of Julius Caesar

ACT III

(Continued from page 69.)

6. censure (sen'shər) *v.* to express strong dis-approval of. ▲ In modern times this word has come to mean "to blame" or "to criti-cize."

■ The state legislature passed a resolution to <u>censure</u> the governor for her misconduct. (Scene 2, line 16)

Original sentence: _____

_____

7. interred (in·turd') *v.* past form of *inter,* which means "to bury." ▲ This word com-bines the prefix *in-,* here meaning "into," and the Latin word *terra,* meaning "earth."

■ The dog quickly <u>interred</u> the beef bone. (Scene 2, line 78)

Original sentence: _____

_____

8. bequeathing (bē·kwēth'ŋ) *v.* present pro-gressive form of *bequeath,* which means "to give by will" or "to hand down." ▲ This word is from the Old English word *becwethan,* having the same definition.

■ The king declared, "When I die, I am be-queathing my gold to my oldest daughter."(Scene 2, line 138)

Original sentence: _____

_____

9. legacy (leg'ə·sē) *n.* inheritance; anything handed down from an ancestor. ▲ This word derives from a Latin word meaning "to send as an ambassador."

■ Sharon's only <u>legacy</u> from her father was a gold watch. (Scene 2, line 138)

Original sentence: _____

_____

10. orator (ôr'ət·ər) *n.* skilled public speaker. ▲ This word is based on a Latin word meaning "to speak."

■ Winston Churchill was awarded the Nobel Prize in literature as much for his accomplish-ments as an <u>orator</u> as for his writing. (Scene 2, line 218)

Original sentence: _____

_____

*Drama Study Guide: **The Tragedy of Julius Caesar***

Literary Elements Worksheet, Act III

Imagery

Imagery is the use of language that appeals to the senses. Most images are word pictures—that is, they appeal to the sense of sight. But images may also appeal to the senses of hearing, smell, touch, or taste. Images of blood almost overwhelm the reader in Act III of *Julius Caesar.*

Understanding Imagery

Read the following passages from *Julius Caesar,* and answer the questions below each passage.

1. "... Stoop, Romans, stoop,
   And let us bathe our hands in Caesar's blood
   Up to the elbows, and besmear our swords.
   Then walk we forth, even to the market place,
   And waving our red weapons o'er our heads,
   Let's all cry 'Peace, freedom, and liberty!'" (Scene 1, lines 105–110)

   a. Which words especially appeal to the sense of sight?

   _____

   b. Which words especially evoke the sense of touch?

   _____

   c. How does Brutus's proposed action make you feel?

   _____

2. With these words, Antony asks Brutus and the others to kill him immediately if they intend to kill him:

   "I do beseech ye, if you bear me hard,
   Now, whilst your purpled hands do reek and smoke,
   Fulfill your pleasure." (Scene 1, lines 157–159)

   a. Which word appeals strongly to the sense of sight?

   _____

   b. Which words evoke the sense of smell?

   _____

(Continued on page 72.)

Drama Study Guide: The Tragedy of Julius Caesar

ACT III

(Continued from page 71.)

Applying Skills

Antony twice compares Caesar's wounds with other parts of the body. Read the images below. Explain the literal meaning of each, and then explain why the image is appropriate.

1. "Had I as many eyes as thou [Caesar] hast wounds,
   Weeping as fast as they stream forth thy blood . . ." (Scene 1, lines 200–201)

   a. The wounds are like _____ because _____.

   _____

   _____

   _____

   b. The image is appropriate because _____

   _____

   _____

   _____

2. "Over thy wounds now do I prophesy
   (Which like dumb mouths do ope their ruby lips
   To beg the voice and utterance of my tongue). . . ." (Scene 1, lines 259–261)

   a. The wounds are like _____ because _____.

   _____

   _____

   _____

   b. The image is appropriate because _____

   _____

   _____

   _____

*Drama Study Guide: **The Tragedy of Julius Caesar***

72

HRW MATERIAL COPYRIGHTED UNDER NOTICE APPEARING EARLIER IN THIS WORK.

Test, Act III

Thoughtful Reading *(40 points)*

On the line provided, write the letter of the *best* answer to each of the following items. *(8 points each)*

_____ 1. Caesar's dying words express surprise at seeing what person among the assassins?

    a. Casca   **b.** Cicero   **c.** Antony   **d.** Brutus

_____ 2. Antony sends a servant to Brutus immediately after Caesar's death to

    a. report that Antony is ill
    b. ask whether Antony can safely speak to Brutus
    c. collect Caesar's body
    d. declare Antony's sympathy with the conspirators

_____ 3. Which of the following is *not* a reason Brutus allows Antony to speak at Caesar's funeral?

    a. Brutus intends to speak first.
    b. Antony has been told what he can and cannot say.
    c. Brutus fears Antony.
    d. Brutus thinks proper rites for Caesar will please the people.

_____ 4. Antony's true purpose in delivering the funeral speech is to

    a. cause unrest over Caesar's assassination
    b. honor Caesar's memory only
    c. read Caesar's will and distribute money to the people
    d. praise the conspirators

_____ 5. The turning point in Act III comes when

    a. Caesar is assassinated
    b. Brutus allows Antony to make the funeral speech
    c. Brutus makes his own speech
    d. Antony speaks at Caesar's funeral

Expanded Response *(30 points)*

6. What adjective *best* characterizes Brutus when he decides to allow Antony to make the funeral oration? On the lines provided, write the letter of the answer you choose and briefly defend your choice. There is more than one possible answer. Use at least one example from the play to support your ideas. *(15 points)*

    a. naive   **b.** idealistic   **c.** just   **d.** scheming

_____

_____

_____

_____

_____

(Continued on page 74.)

Drama Study Guide: The Tragedy of Julius Caesar

ACT III

(Continued from page 73.)

7. In Scene 3, Cinna the poet is brutally murdered. In the chart below, list three purposes this scene serves. Consider the following in forming your answer: the effects of Antony's speech, what is likely to happen during the remainder of the play, and the role of language in politics. *(15 points)*

Purposes of Scene 3		
1.	2.	3.

Written Response *(30 points)*

8. In Scene 2, Antony turns a shocked, confused crowd of mourners into an angry mob of rioters. On the lines provided, write a paragraph describing at least three specific ways in which Antony achieves this effect.

_____

_____

_____

_____

_____

_____

_____

_____

_____

_____

*Drama Study Guide: **The Tragedy of Julius Caesar***

Graphic Organizer for Active Reading, Act IV

Who Is Cassius?

At the beginning of Act IV, Scene 3, Brutus is angry with Cassius and makes several accusations against him. What are they? Create a "Wanted" poster for Cassius by filling in the lines below.

Wanted: Cassius

Physical Description: _____
_____
_____

Crimes: _____
_____
_____
_____

Brief History: _____
_____
_____

Personality Traits: _____
_____
_____

Attitude Toward Government: _____
_____
_____
_____

ACT IV

1. How have Brutus's feelings changed by the end of Scene 3? _____
_____
_____

2. How have your feelings about Cassius changed through the play so far? _____
_____
_____

Drama Study Guide: The Tragedy of Julius Caesar

Making Meanings, Act IV

First Thoughts

1. Whose behavior surprises you in this act? Why? How do you feel about this character now?

Shaping Interpretations

2. How is Antony **characterized** by his words and actions in Scene 1? In your opinion, is the Antony we see in this scene consistent with the Antony we saw earlier?

3. If you were staging the play, how would you let your audience know that in Scene 2 the location has changed (instead of a house in Rome, the set is now a battlefield)?

4. In drama, relationships burst open under pressure and reveal certain truths. After the burst the relationship is either renewed or ended. Brutus and Cassius have been friends throughout the play, with Cassius clearly the subordinate. In Scene 3, they quarrel. How is their **conflict** resolved? What has become of their relationship by the end of the scene?

Reviewing the Text

a. Describe the military situation presented in Act IV. What is going on between the conspirators and the triumvirate?

b. As Scene 1 opens, what are Antony, Octavius, and Lepidus doing? What breach has opened among them?

c. Why is Brutus uneasy at the beginning of Scene 2?

d. What are the issues that cause Brutus and Cassius to quarrel in Scene 3?

e. According to Brutus, what were the reasons for Portia's death? How does he respond to her death?

f. What vision does Brutus see at the end of Act IV?

5. In what ways does the meeting of the conspirators in Scene 3 parallel the meeting of the triumvirate in Scene 1? In what ways are the scenes different?

6. The scene with Cassius shows a harsh Brutus. What kind of Brutus appears with Lucius and the guards?

7. As the director of the play, you would have to make a decision about how to represent the ghost. You could have someone play the ghost, or you could just use a voice. What would each of these choices suggest about whether or not the ghost is real? What might the ghost represent to Brutus?

Connecting with the Text

8. Which **character** do you most sympathize with by the end of Act IV? Why?

9. In lines 141–159 of Scene 3, Brutus and Cassius display different reactions to Portia's death. Why are their reactions different? How do you feel about these men now?

10. Think about the two groups preparing for war here. Which side would you want to be on? Why?

Choices: Building Your Portfolio, Act IV

Creative Writing/Speaking

A Boy's View

If you were young Lucius, what would you think about the events you've observed? How would you feel about Brutus? Write Lucius's thoughts and fears in a journal entry. Be sure to date the entry, and have Lucius tell where he is while he is writing. You might deliver your account aloud to the class.

Language Link Mini-Lesson, Act IV

Anachronisms

An **anachronism** (ə·nak′rə·niz′əm) (from *ana-*, "against," and *chronos,* "time") is a chronologically displaced event, detail, word, or phrase in a literary work. A car in a story about the Civil War would be an anachronism; cars had not yet been invented. In a play set in the 1920s, the word *nerd* would be an anachronism. *Nerd* wasn't used as slang until much later in the twentieth century.

   Remember that *Julius Caesar* is set in 44–43 B.C. in ancient Rome. Do you see anachronisms in these passages?

1. ". . . He plucked me ope his doublet and offered them his throat to cut."
   (Act 1, Scene 2, lines 263–264)

2. "Peace! Count the clock."

   "The clock hath stricken three." (Act II, Scene 1, line 192)

3. "Look, Lucius, here's the book I sought for so; / I put it in the pocket of my gown."
   (Act IV, Scene 3, lines 249–250)

Try It Out

➤ Find the one word in each passage at the left that is "out of time."

➤ Suppose Shakespeare wanted to correct his errors. How could he eliminate the anachronisms?

➤ Make a class list of other situations that would be anachronistic. An example might be the conspirators' use of guns instead of daggers to kill Caesar or Brutus's receipt of a telegram telling him of Portia's death.

ACT IV

Drama Study Guide: The Tragedy of Julius Caesar

Words to Own Worksheet, Act IV

Developing Vocabulary

Carefully read each word's definition, explanation, and sample sentence. The definition and the sample sentence are based on the word as it is used in *Julius Caesar*. Many of these definitions are now archaic. Write a sentence of your own using the word.

1. **chastisement** (chas′tīz·mənt) *n.* punishment; reprimand. ▲ This word derives from a Latin word meaning "pure."

■ Ms. Swan's chastisement of the class was so mild that several students did not realize they were being scolded. (Scene 3, line 16)

Original sentence: _____

_____

2. **contaminate** (kən·tam′ə·nāt′) *v.* to make impure; to pollute. ▲ *Contaminate* is based on the prefix *com-,* which here means "together," and the Latin word *tangere,* which means "to touch."

■ Bacteria from an upstream sewage treatment plant will contaminate the river on which the town depends for water. (Scene 3, line 24)

Original sentence: _____

_____

3. **bait** (bāt) *v.* to torment; to tease. ▲ *Bait* comes from an Old Norse word meaning "to bite."

■ I can always bait my uncle Loren with a critical comment about his political party. (Scene 3, line 28)

Original sentence: _____

_____

4. **choleric** (käl′ər·ik) *adj.* irritable; quick-tempered. ▲ This word is based on the Greek word for *bile.* In medieval times, bile, a substance secreted by the liver, was thought to be the source of emotions, including anger.

■ By nature, Shawn is rather choleric, but his brother is always amiable and even-tempered. (Scene 3, line 43)

Original sentence: _____

_____

5. **covetous** (kuv′ət·əs) *adj.* greedy. ▲ Although *covetous* and *greedy* are synonyms, *covetous* implies desiring something that someone else has.

■ On her birthday, Beth becomes covetous, wanting even more gifts than she receives. (Scene 3, line 79)

Original sentence: _____

_____

(Continued on page 79.)

*Drama Study Guide: **The Tragedy of Julius Caesar***

(Continued from page 78.)

6. rash (rash) *adj.* reckless; incautious. ▲ This word can also mean "a large number," as in "a rash of accidents."

■ Jed's rash behavior almost cost him his job. (Scene 3, line 119)

Original sentence: _____

_____

7. nimbleness (nim′bəl·nis) *n.* lightness and speed in movement; agility. ▲ This word can also mean "mental quickness."

■ Considerable nimbleness is required to do gymnastics well. (Scene 3, line 199)

Original sentence: _____

_____

8. venture (ven′chər) *n.* chance; fortune. ▲ This word is a shortened term for *adventure*. It also means "a risky or dangerous undertaking."

■ To invest money in such a business would be a worthwhile venture. (Scene 3, line 221)

Original sentence: _____

_____

9. repose (ri·pōz′) *n.* sleep; rest. ▲ This word can also mean "peace of mind."

■ The man's repose was interrupted by the arrival of his grandchildren. (Scene 3, line 230)

Original sentence: _____

_____

10. apparition (ap′ə·rish′ən) *n.* strange figure that appears suddenly; ghost. ▲ The Latin word on which *apparition* is based means "to appear."

■ People who have stayed in the old hotel claim to have seen an apparition moving through the hallways at night. (Scene 3, line 274)

Original sentence: _____

_____

ACT IV

*Drama Study Guide: **The Tragedy of Julius Caesar***

HRW MATERIAL COPYRIGHTED UNDER NOTICE APPEARING EARLIER IN THIS WORK.

79

Literary Elements Worksheet, Act IV

Conflict

Conflict is a struggle or clash between opposing characters, forces, or emotions. In an **external conflict** a character struggles against an outside force—another character, a social group, a force of nature, or even a force from some supernatural realm. **Internal conflict** is the struggle between opposing needs, desires, or emotions within a character.

Understanding Conflict

On the line to the left of each item below, write the letter of the type of conflict shown by each event from Act IV of *Julius Caesar*. Some answers are used twice.

a. Person versus self

b. Person versus the supernatural

c. Person versus person

d. Group versus group

_____ **1.** The armies of Brutus and Cassius are opposed by those of Antony, Octavius, and Lepidus.

_____ **2.** Cassius and Brutus argue so bitterly that Cassius offers to let Brutus stab him.

_____ **3.** Brutus's wife, Portia, is so depressed over events that she commits suicide.

_____ **4.** Brutus confronts the ghost of Caesar.

_____ **5.** The people are beginning to oppose the armies of Brutus and Cassius.

_____ **6.** Brutus is so troubled that he misplaces things.

Applying Skills

In Scene 3 of Act IV, conflict erupts when Brutus and Cassius, who have long been friends, quarrel violently. Label each statement *T* if true or *F* if false in the blanks at the left.

_____ **1.** The two men restrain themselves and avoid showing their anger openly.

_____ **2.** Brutus accuses Cassius of handling bribes.

_____ **3.** Brutus calls Cassius a "slight man" and a "madman."

_____ **4.** Cassius points out that Brutus is the older of the two men.

_____ **5.** Brutus claims that Cassius deprived him of funds.

_____ **6.** Cassius draws his dagger.

_____ **7.** Brutus strikes Cassius.

_____ **8.** Cassius becomes sympathetic when he learns that Brutus's wife is dead.

_____ **9.** Their anger vented, both men apologize.

(Continued on page 81.)

Drama Study Guide: The Tragedy of Julius Caesar

80

HRW MATERIAL COPYRIGHTED UNDER NOTICE APPEARING EARLIER IN THIS WORK.

(Continued from page 80.)

_____ **10.** The conflict is resolved at least in part because each man genuinely respects the other.

_____ **11.** Cassius defers to Brutus's judgment as to how the next battle should be fought.

Reader's Response

The violence of the open conflict between Cassius and Brutus arouses many feelings and reactions in readers and viewers. Circle the reactions you felt at various stages of the quarrel.

annoyance	confusion	calmness	curiosity
fear	nervousness	recognition	suspense
sympathy	tension	understanding	worry

ACT IV

Test, Act IV

Thoughtful Reading (40 points)

On the line provided, write the letter of the *best* answer to each of the following items. *(8 points each)*

_____ **1.** The military conflict in Act IV takes place between

    a. Antony-Brutus and Lepidus-Octavius
    b. Brutus-Cassius and Antony-Octavius
    c. Brutus and Cassius
    d. Antony and Octavius

_____ **2.** Brutus is motivated mainly by thoughts of

    a. honor
    b. friendship
    c. power
    d. Rome

_____ **3.** By his treatment of Cassius, Brutus gives the impression that he is

    a. arrogant and condescending
    b. cynical and punishing
    c. carefree and fun loving
    d. righteous but forgiving

_____ **4.** In his attitude toward Lepidus, Antony reveals himself to be

    a. honest
    b. foolish
    c. arrogant
    d. indecisive

_____ **5.** Before the battle of Philippi, Brutus tells Cassius:

    "There is a tide in the affairs of men
    Which, taken at the flood, leads on to fortune;
    Omitted, all the voyage of their life
    Is bound in shallows and in miseries." (Scene 3, lines 215–218)

Brutus means that

    a. success depends on seizing the timely opportunity
    b. fate is inescapable
    c. fortune is fickle
    d. hasty action brings certain defeat

(Continued on page 83.)

*Drama Study Guide: **The Tragedy of Julius Caesar***

(Continued from page 82.)

Expanded Response *(30 points)*

6. Imagine that you are to direct this play. Choose two very tense moments in Act IV and describe what you would like to see on the stage at those moments. *(15 points)*

Moment	Placement of Actors	Props	Lighting
a.			
b.			

7. Brutus and Cassius's relationship is a complicated one involving their personal, political, and military roles. Which aspect of their relationship has the *greatest* impact on their argument in Scene 3? On the lines provided, write the letter of the answer you choose and briefly defend your choice. There is more than one possible answer. Use at least one example from the play to support your ideas. *(15 points)*

a. generals planning for battle   **c.** political thinkers
b. old and close friends   **d.** co-conspirators

_____

_____

_____

_____

Written Response *(30 points)*

8. The ghost of Julius Caesar appears at the end of Act IV. What function do you think the ghost serves in the play? Are we prepared for it by anything that is said earlier? On a separate sheet of paper, write a paragraph describing your interpretation of the ghost scene. Use at least two examples from the play to support your ideas.

Drama Study Guide: The Tragedy of Julius Caesar

ACT IV

Graphic Organizer for Active Reading, Act V

Who's Who Now?

In the outlines below, write your final evaluation of the characters of Antony, Brutus, and Cassius based on their actions in the last act. Include at least one quotation from the act to support your opinion.

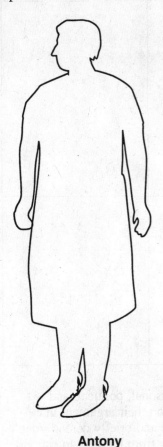

Antony

Brutus

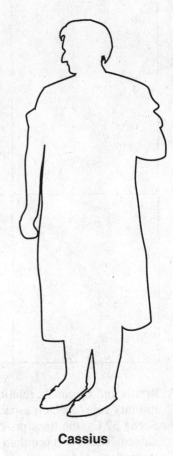

Cassius

1. At the end of the play, which of the three characters do you admire most? Why?

_____

_____

_____

_____

2. Which do you consider the most villainous? Why?

_____

_____

_____

_____

*Drama Study Guide: **The Tragedy of Julius Caesar***

Making Meanings, Act V

First Thoughts

1. How do you feel about what happens to Brutus and Cassius?

Shaping Interpretations

2. Why is it significant that Octavius delivers the play's final speech?

3. Identify at least three examples of **irony** in Scene 3, Cassius's death scene. How do these ironies make you feel?

4. Look at Scenes 3 and 5 and the dying words of Cassius and Brutus. How does each man view Caesar's murder? Do you think each man had a choice other than suicide? Explain.

5. Brutus makes two mistakes—one in Act II and one in Act III—that stem from his idealized vision of the assassination and his self-image as an "honorable man." What are these errors, and how do they lead to Brutus's downfall?

6. Describe your final view of Brutus and the choices he made. Did he misread the evidence that Caesar might become a dictator? Should he have betrayed a friend for the public good? Was he wrong to kill the only man who could bring order out of chaos? Support your responses with evidence from the play.

7. Critics argue that Julius Caesar dominates the play (Cassius says in Act I that he "doth bestride the narrow world / Like a Colossus . . ."). How would you defend this view? How is Caesar "present" in the second half of the play?

8. In his essay *The Poetics,* Aristotle described the **tragic hero** as a person more noble than evil, whose fortunes go from good to bad. Does Brutus fit this description, or is the tragic hero someone else, perhaps Caesar? Or does the play lack a tragic hero? Defend your answer.

Extending the Text

9. Few words inspired such anxiety in the ancient Romans as the word *king.* Do you think the anxieties of Brutus and others about Caesar's potential "kingship" were justified? How do you think Shakespeare's audience, living under the strong and stable monarchy of the aging Queen Elizabeth I, might have felt about choosing between dictatorship and anarchy? How do you think American audiences of today feel about this issue?

Reviewing the Text

a. Which four characters finally confront one another in Scene 1 of Act V?

b. What are the results of the first round of battle at Philippi? In the end, who triumphs over whom?

c. What mistaken assumptions lead to Cassius's death?

d. Why does Brutus think he must commit suicide?

e. How do Antony and Octavius react to Brutus's death?

ACT V

Drama Study Guide: The Tragedy of Julius Caesar

Choices: Building Your Portfolio, Act V

Critical Writing

1. Updating Characters

If Cassius, Brutus, Antony, and Caesar were living today, what do you imagine their beliefs, life styles and career ambitions would be? Think of yourself as a journalist, and write a brief profile of each of these characters for a national magazine.

Creative Writing

2. Extending the Story

Some contemporary writers have taken portions of older plays (or novels) and expanded on small episodes to make entirely new works of literature. Choose an episode in this play, and explain how it might be expanded into a play or story of its own. You might consider these scenes:

a. Portia's suicide

b. Caesar's last evening alive

c. the discovery of Cinna's body

d. Calphurnia's response to Caesar's murder

Critical Writing

3. Responding to a Critic

In Act V, Titinius, despairing over Cassius's death, cries, "Alas, thou hast misconstrued everything!" According to the critic Marjorie Garber, "That one cry . . . might well serve as an epigraph for the whole of *Julius Caesar*." Do you agree with Garber's view? Have any characters in the play other than Cassius fatally misconstrued or misunderstood actions or words? Write a response to Garber's statement. Tell whether or not you agree with it. Then, cite evidence from the text that upholds or refutes Garber's thesis.

Art

4. Set Design

Imagine that you are the set designer for a production of *Julius Caesar*. Choose one of the key scenes of the play, such as one of the funeral orations or the death of Cassius or Brutus. Design and draw a set for the scene, indicating scenery and props.

Creative Writing

5. Another Ending

Suppose Brutus does not die but is captured and brought before Octavius and Antony. Choose one or more partners, and use what you know about these characters to develop and write a scene in which Brutus's fate is decided. Will the victors execute or exile Brutus or carry him back to Rome in chains, as Cassius predicted? Will Brutus plead for his life? Will Antony or Octavius show mercy? Will they offer Brutus a share of the power? After you've written your ending to the play, consider presenting it to your class.

Critical Writing

6. Analyzing a Character

In a brief essay, write a character analysis of Brutus. Use one of the critical comments below as your thesis statement. Be sure to use details from the play to support what the critic says.

> *Brutus is humorlessly good. If his duty is to know himself, his performance fails. Nobility has numbed him until he cannot see himself for his principles. When his principles are expressing themselves, they are beautiful in their clarity. . . . But when he speaks to himself he knows not who is there; he addresses a strange audience, and fumbles. . . . He is not mad or haunted or inspired or perplexed in the extreme. He is simply confused.*
>
> —Mark Van Doren

> *Brutus is an intellectual who can do things, who is not . . . hampered by doubts. He can do things—but he always does them wrong: His advice is invariably fatal, from the moment of the murder down to the Battle of Philippi. He cannot realize that men seek their own interests, for he has never sought his own, he has lived nobly among noble thoughts, wedded to a noble wife. He is kind to his servant. Everything he does is touched with fineness. Yet Brutus is not frigid. He just avoids being a prig. We are able to take him to our hearts.*
>
> —E. M. Forster

(Continued on page 87.)

*Drama Study Guide: **The Tragedy of Julius Caesar***

(Continued from page 86.)

Critical Thinking/Art

7. A Power Line

Many readers see this as a play about power and its shifts from one faction or individual to others. Draw a graph tracing the shifts of power in the play. Begin with the situation in the opening scene of Act I, and follow the exchange of power through each of the following scenes and acts. You might want to illustrate your graph. Be sure to supply dates whenever you can.

Critical Writing

8. Then and Now

In *Julius Caesar* you have seen the results of the political chaos caused by the assassination of Caesar and the battles for power that followed. Write a brief essay in which you compare and contrast politics today (national, state, or local) with the political scene Shakespeare described.

Critical Writing

9. Going to the Source

On pages 133–136 of the HRW Classics edition of *Julius Caesar,* you'll find an excerpt from Plutarch's *Life of Caesar.* In a brief essay, compare details in Plutarch's work with details from the equivalent scenes in Shakespeare's play. What do you think of Shakespeare's changes in the story?

Critical Writing

10. Staging the Play

John Mason Brown's review, "*Julius Caesar* in an Absorbing Production" (pages 140–144 of the HRW Classics edition of *Julius Caesar*), describes a famous modern-dress version of the play that was directed by Orson Welles. The review praises the production for showing that the play's themes are timeless. If you were asked to direct a film version of the play, what setting would you choose—the original ancient Rome or a more recent one? Whom would you cast in the major roles—Caesar, Cassius, Brutus, Antony,

and Portia? Write a "treatment" like the ones directors prepare for studio heads, in which you describe the setting you've chosen and list the actors you're interested in (and say why they'd be perfect to breathe life into these classic roles). Make sure to defend your choices.

Research

11. Assassinations/History

On pages 145–147 of the HRW Classics edition of *Julius Caesar,* you'll find an article describing one of the most tragic events in U.S. history— the assassination of President John F. Kennedy. Like Julius Caesar, Kennedy was a popular leader, and his death devastated Americans. You now know from Shakespeare's play how the Romans reacted to Caesar's death. There was rioting, infighting, and chaos. Choose another leader who was assassinated (Martin Luther King, Jr., Mohandas Gandhi, or Abraham Lincoln, for example). Research the event, using encyclopedias and the Internet. The reference section of your library might even have microfilm of relevant newspapers. Why was the leader you chose assassinated? Is there some mystery involved? How did people react to the death? Were their responses peaceful or destructive? Once you've found some answers, prepare a brief oral report to present to your classmates.

Critical Writing

12. An Editorial

On pages 148–151 of the HRW Classics edition of *Julius Caesar,* you'll find Jimmy Breslin's feature article about the riots that followed the assassination of Martin Luther King, Jr. Write an editorial on these riots, using the Breslin article as a source, or on the assassination of Julius Caesar as you understand it from Shakespeare's play. Remember, an editorial writer takes a stand, commenting on the events he or she is writing about. Take a stand on Caesar's assassination or the riots that followed King's death. Who was to blame? Was the action justified? What were the aftereffects? Could the event have been avoided?

ACT V

Drama Study Guide: The Tragedy of Julius Caesar

Language Link Mini-Lesson, Act V

Famous Passages: Make Them Yours

Memorizing isn't hard work, and the rewards are worth the effort. If you memorize one or more of these famous speeches now, you'll find yourself remembering them years later—and even finding occasions to *use* them.

One way to memorize speeches easily is to use the "bricklayer" method. The term means that, like a bricklayer, who lays down row upon row of bricks, an actor memorizes lines by building one line upon another.

Try It Out

Choose at least one of the long speeches and one of the short speeches. Using the technique summarized at the left, memorize both speeches. In a small group, share your interpretations of the speeches, and discuss occasions in life when it would be appropriate to quote each speech. For example, which lines might be quoted if you were a police officer assigned a dangerous beat?

Read the first line of a speech until you can say it without looking at it. Then, read that line and the next line until you can say the first two lines without looking at them. Continue until you can say the whole speech without looking at it. Then, you can work on interpretation and presentation.

1. "Why, man, he doth bestride the narrow world
   Like a Colossus, and we petty men
   Walk under his huge legs and peep about
   To find ourselves dishonorable graves.
   Men at some time are masters of their fates:
   The fault, dear Brutus, is not in our stars,
   But in ourselves, that we are underlings." (Act I, Scene 2, lines 135–141)

2. "Cowards die many times before their deaths;
   The valiant never taste of death but once.
   Of all the wonders that I yet have heard,
   It seems to me most strange that men should fear,
   Seeing that death, a necessary end,
   Will come when it will come." (Act II, Scene 2, lines 32–37)

3. "The evil that men do lives after them,
   The good is oft interrèd with their bones. . . ." (Act III, Scene 2, lines 77–78)

4. "There is a tide in the affairs of men
   Which, taken at the flood, leads on to fortune;
   Omitted, all the voyage of their life
   Is bound in shallows and in miseries.
   On such a full sea are we now afloat,
   And we must take the current when it serves,
   Or lose our ventures." (Act IV, Scene 3, lines 215–221)

*Drama Study Guide: **The Tragedy of Julius Caesar***

Words to Own Worksheet, Act V

Developing Vocabulary

Carefully read each word's definition, explanation, and sample sentence. The definition and the sample sentence are based on the meaning of the word as it is used in *Julius Caesar*. Many of these definitions are now archaic. Write a sentence of your own using the word.

1. **parley** (pär′lē) *n.* conference or discussion, especially with an enemy. ▲ *Parley* is based on the French word *parler,* meaning "to speak." Do not confuse *parley* with *parlay,* which means "to maneuver an asset to great advantage."

■ The two sides held a parley that lasted several weeks before a truce was worked out. (Scene 1, line 21)

Original sentence: _____

_____

2. **vile** (vīl) *adj.* evil; offensive. ▲ This word is derived from a Latin word meaning "cheap" or "base."

■ Murder is considered one of the most vile acts a human being can commit. (Scene 1, line 39)

Original sentence: _____

_____

3. **cur** (kʉr) *n.* mean or contemptible person. ▲ Another meaning of this word is "dog of mixed breed."

■ When the debate became heated, one of the candidates called the other a cur. (Scene 1, line 43)

Original sentence: _____

_____

4. **legions** (lē′jənz) *n. pl.* large groups of soldiers. ▲ In Roman history a legion comprised three thousand to six thousand foot soldiers, with additional cavalry.

■ The barbarians were turned back by the Roman legions. (Scene 2, line 2)

Original sentence: _____

_____

5. **disconsolate** (dis·kän′sə·lit) *adj.* so unhappy that nothing will comfort. ▲ The root of this word is also found in *console* ("to comfort") and *inconsolable* ("unable to be comforted").

■ When his puppy was hit by a car, Manuel was disconsolate for days. (Scene 3, line 55)

Original sentence: _____

_____

ACT V

(Continued on page 90.)

Drama Study Guide: The Tragedy of Julius Caesar

(Continued from page 89.)

6. misconstrued (mis′kən·strōōd′) *v.* past form of *misconstrue,* which means "to misunderstand; to misinterpret." ▲ The prefix *mis-* means "wrong" or "wrongly."

■ Your sister has <u>misconstrued</u> my remark, and now she is unnecessarily angry with me. (Scene 3, line 84)

Original sentence: _____

_____

7. entrails (en′trālz) *n. pl.* inner organs, specifically the intestines. ▲ The Latin word from which *entrails* is derived means "internal."

■ The lion cubs gnawed contentedly on the <u>entrails</u> of the antelope their mother had killed. (Scene 3, line 96)

Original sentence: _____

_____

8. tarrying (tar′ē·iŋ) *n.* the act of lingering; delaying. ▲ This word and *tardy* come from a Latin word that means "to delay."

■ "There can be no <u>tarrying</u> if we are going to get to the museum before it closes," the teacher told her class. (Scene 5, line 30)

Original sentence: _____

_____

9. bondage (bän′dij) *n.* slavery; servitude. ▲ The suffix *-age* adds the meaning "act," "condition," or "result of" to the word to which it is attached.

■ Many spirituals compare the plight of African slaves in America to the <u>bondage</u> of the Israelites in Egypt. (Scene 5, line 54)

Original sentence: _____

_____

10. bestow (bē·stō′) *v.* to apply; to devote. ▲ In modern usage this word usually means "to present as a gift" and is followed by *on* or *upon.*

■ "Dear son, do <u>bestow</u> thy last days upon me before the voyage," said the father. (Scene 5, line 61)

Original sentence: _____

_____

Drama Study Guide: **The Tragedy of Julius Caesar**

Language Link Worksheet, Act V

Famous Passages: Make Them Yours

Delivering a speech from Shakespeare can be an exciting and enjoyable way to make a play your own. Once you have chosen a speech to present orally, be sure you understand its meaning and the emotion it is meant to express. Then, consider *how* you will deliver the speech. What words or phrases will you emphasize? Where will you pause? You can mark the text of the speech to indicate how you will deliver it. The chart below gives a description of the kinds of markings some speakers use when planning their delivery. Use them to mark the speech you have chosen to present.

Where to Mark	Kind of Marks	Delivery Technique
at commas, semicolons, colons, dashes, and periods (to indicate length of pause)	use one slash (/) for a short pause, two slashes (//) for a longer pause	vary length of pause to match punctuation
words in parentheses	highlight in color or underline	pause and lower volume
words in italics	highlight in color or underline	use higher volume to emphasize or stress
question marks	use an upward pointing arrow to show rising inflection	raise voice where arrow indicates
meaningful word groups, repeated phrases	underline or highlight in color	change tone, volume, or rate of speech to emphasize
parenthetical phrases	mark with parentheses or highlight in color	pause and lower volume
unfamiliar words	provide phonetic spelling	deliver as required by context
at the end of one line of poetry and the beginning of the next line	draw a curved line joining the two lines	do not pause between the two lines

EXERCISE A Reading a Marked Manuscript

Read the following marked manuscripts aloud, referring to the chart for clarification of markings. Then, answer the questions that follow each passage.

> **Cassius.** Flatterers! Now, (Brutus), thank yourself; /
>
>   This tongue had not offended so today,
>   If Cassius might have ruled.
>
>   —Act V, Scene 1, lines 45–47

1. How should the words *flatterers* and *Cassius* be delivered? _____

_____

2. Why is the word *Brutus* in line 45 in parentheses? _____

_____

(Continued on page 92.)

Drama Study Guide: The Tragedy of Julius Caesar

ACT V

(Continued from page 91.)

3. What does the slash indicate at the end of line 45? _____

_____

    Brutus.   Are yet two Romans living such as these // ↑

               The <u>last</u> of all the Romans, / fare thee well! //

               It is <u>impossible</u> that ever Rome

               Should breed thy fellow. // (Friends), I owe moe tears

               To this dead man than you shall see me pay. //

               I shall find time, / Cassius; // <u>I shall find time.</u>

               <u>Come</u> therefore, / and to Thasos send his body; //

               His funerals shall not be in our camp,

               Lest it discomfort us. //

                          —Act V, Scene 3, lines 98–106

4. With what word should the rising inflection begin? _____

5. What do the long curving lines indicate? _____

6. How should *friends* in line 101 be delivered? _____

7. Why is the phrase "I shall find time" in line 103 underscored? _____

8. Why is no slash indicated at the end of the second to last line? _____

EXERCISE B   **Marking a Passage for Delivery**

Mark the following passage for oral delivery. Then, memorize it, practice your delivery, and present it to your classmates or family.

    Antony.   This was the noblest Roman of them all.

               All the conspirators, save only he

               Did that they did in envy of great Caesar;

               He, only in a general honest thought

               And common good to all, made one of them.

               His life was gentle, and the elements

               So mixed in him that Nature might stand up

               And say to all the world, "This was a man!"

                        —Act V, Scene 5, lines 68–75

*Drama Study Guide: **The Tragedy of Julius Caesar***

92   HRW MATERIAL COPYRIGHTED UNDER NOTICE APPEARING EARLIER IN THIS WORK.

Literary Elements Worksheet, Act V

The Tragic Hero

A **tragic hero** is the main character of a tragedy, a play in which the hero comes to an unhappy end. A tragic hero is usually dignified, courageous, and high ranking. The hero's downfall is caused by a tragic flaw (character weakness) or by forces beyond his or her control. Such a hero usually wins some self-knowledge and wisdom, despite defeat or even death.

Understanding the Tragic Hero

Does *Julius Caesar* have a tragic hero? Fill in the chart to help you decide whether Caesar or Brutus has most of the defining characteristics of the tragic hero, or whether they both have them.

Characteristic	Julius Caesar	Brutus
is the main character		
shows evidence of high rank		
shows nobility of character		
is marred by tragic flaw or fatal mistake in judgment		
gains self-knowledge and wisdom		
comes to an unhappy end		

(Continued on page 94.)

ACT V

Drama Study Guide: The Tragedy of Julius Caesar

(Continued from page 93.)

Applying Skills

On the basis of your completed chart, choose one of these topic sentences, and then list the details that support it.

a. The play *Julius Caesar* has no true tragic hero.

b. Julius Caesar is the tragic hero of the play.

c. Brutus is the tragic hero of the play.

_____

_____

_____

_____

_____

_____

_____

_____

_____

_____

_____

_____

_____

_____

_____

Reader's Response

Whether or not readers consider Brutus a tragic hero, they usually have strong feelings about his character and the choices he makes. Considering the play as a whole, how do you feel about Brutus? Circle the words you would apply to his character.

ambitious	admirable	brave	cowardly
criminal	honest	immoral	loyal
misguided	noble	patriotic	troubled
trusting	underhanded	unwise	weak

Drama Study Guide: ***The Tragedy of Julius Caesar***

Test, Act V

Thoughtful Reading (40 points)

On the line provided, write the letter of the *best* answer to each of the following items. *(8 points each)*

_____ 1. All of the action in Act V takes place during what period of time?

    a. a single day   **c.** about a week
    b. two days   **d.** over a month

_____ 2. "This was the noblest Roman of them all." The punctuation of the preceding line indicates that it is

    a. an iambic pentameter line   **c.** an end-stopped line
    b. a run-on line   **d.** a rhymed line

_____ 3. Shakespeare's use of minor characters to report on the battle's progress helps to create

    a. unbiased reporting   **c.** horror
    b. comedy   **d.** suspense

_____ 4. How does Pindarus misread what happens on the battlefield?

    a. He thinks Titinius is killed.   **c.** He thinks Titinius is captured.
    b. He thinks the battle is lost.   **d.** He thinks Brutus has surrendered.

_____ 5. What does Cassius say is avenged by his death?

    a. Portia's death   **c.** Brutus's death
    b. Caesar's death   **d.** his own errors

Expanded Response (30 points)

6. At the end of the play, Octavius speaks of "the glories of this happy day." What other word from the list below *best* characterizes the day's events? On the lines provided, write the letter of the answer you choose and briefly defend your choice. There is more than one possible answer. Use at least one example from the play to support your ideas. *(15 points)*

    a. revenge   **b.** order   **c.** honor

_____

_____

_____

_____

_____

_____

_____

_____

ACT V

(Continued on page 96.)

Drama Study Guide: The Tragedy of Julius Caesar

(Continued from page 95.)

7. Remember that a tragic hero is someone who is noble but whose fortunes go from good to bad. In the chart below, list reasons why Brutus and Caesar may or may not be considered tragic heroes. *(15 points)*

	Tragic	Not Tragic
Brutus		
Caesar		

Written Response *(30 points)*

8. In Act I, Brutus tells Cassius that though he would not have Caesar for a king, he still loves him. Throughout the play, characters express what seem to be contradictory feelings or act in apparent contradiction to their own professed beliefs. On the lines below, write a paragraph in which you explore at least two examples of contradictory feelings or actions in the last act.

_____

_____

_____

_____

_____

_____

_____

_____

_____

_____

*Drama Study Guide: **The Tragedy of Julius Caesar***

Test, the Play as a Whole

Responding to Literature *(70 points)*

For items 1 and 2 below, choose a character from the following list and apply the activity to that character. *(10 points each)*

Caesar   Brutus   Cassius   Antony

1. At several points in the play, a character has to make an important decision. Using the chart below, choose a character, identify a choice that character has to make, explain why he makes that choice, and then list the consequences of his decision.

Character: _____

Choice	Reason	Consequences

2. The characters in the play act according to different philosophies of life. Using the chart below, describe one character's philosophy or values, and then explain how that philosophy motivates one of that character's actions.

Character: _____

Philosophy	Action

(Continued on page 98.)

*Drama Study Guide: **The Tragedy of Julius Caesar***

(Continued from page 97.)

Respond to each of the questions below. Use an extra sheet of paper if necessary. *(25 points each)*

3. Choose one scene in the play, and describe how Shakespeare gives the audience a sense of the setting through the language and the action.

_____

_____

_____

_____

_____

_____

_____

_____

_____

_____

_____

4. Several passions are dramatized in *The Tragedy of Julius Caesar.* Choose one of them, and write a paragraph about how that passion is illustrated in the action of the play. Support your argument by referring to two scenes in which that passion is particularly evident.

_____

_____

_____

_____

_____

_____

_____

_____

_____

_____

_____

_____

(Continued on page 99.)

*Drama Study Guide: **The Tragedy of Julius Caesar***

(Continued from page 98.)

Paraphrasing *(30 points)*

Read the following passages in their contexts, and then paraphrase each one—that is, rephrase each passage in your own words. If you find a word you do not know, use context clues or the footnotes in the play to help you figure out what it means. A sample is done for you. *(10 points each)*

Cassius.
The fault, dear Brutus, is not in our stars,
But in ourselves, that we are underlings.
      —Act I, Scene 2, lines 140–141

We have no one to blame but ourselves, dear Brutus, if we act like

Caesar's inferiors.

5. **Caesar.**
   Cowards die many times before their deaths;
   The valiant never taste of death but once.
        —Act II, Scene 2, lines 32–33

6. **Antony.**
   For Brutus, as you know, was Caesar's angel.
        —Act III, Scene 2, line 182

7. **Antony.**
   The evil that men do lives after them,
   The good is oft interrèd with their bones.
        —Act III, Scene 2, lines 77–78

*Drama Study Guide: **The Tragedy of Julius Caesar***

Testing the Genre

Reading a Shakespearean Drama

Carefully read the excerpt below from Act I, Scene 7, of Shakespeare's well-known play *The Tragedy of Macbeth*. Then, answer the questions that follow.

After Macbeth has won a great battle, King Duncan visits his castle to reward him by naming him Thane (Chief) of Cawdor. Macbeth, however, is not content with his new title. He wishes to be king. Lady Macbeth is even more ambitious than her husband. She wants him to murder King Duncan and claim the crown.

[*Enter Lady Macbeth.*]		
Macbeth.	How now! What news?	
Lady Macbeth.	He has almost supped. Why have you left the chamber?	
Macbeth.	Hath he asked for me?	
Lady Macbeth.	Know you not he has?	
Macbeth.	We will proceed no further in this business:	
	He hath honored me of late, and I have bought	5
	Golden opinions from all sorts of people,	
	Which would be worn now in their newest gloss,	
	Not cast aside so soon.	
Lady Macbeth.	Was the hope drunk	
	Wherein you dressed yourself? Hath it slept since,	
	And wakes it now, to look so green and pale	10
	At what it did so freely? From this time	
	Such I account thy love. Art thou afeard	
	To be the same in thine own act and <u>valor</u>	
	As thou art in desire? Wouldst thou have that	
	Which thou esteem'st the ornament of life,	15
	And live a coward in thine own esteem,	
	Letting "I dare not" wait upon "I would,"	
	Like the poor cat i' th' adage?	
Macbeth.	<u>Prithee</u>, peace.	
	I dare do all that may become a man;	
	Who dares do more is none.	
Lady Macbeth.	What beast was't then	20
	That made you break this <u>enterprise</u> to me?	
	When you durst do it, then you were a man;	
	And to be more than what you were, you would	
	Be so much more the man. Nor time nor place	
	Did then adhere, and yet you would make both.	25
	They have made themselves, and that their fitness now	
	Does unmake you. I have given suck, and know	
	How tender 'tis to love the babe that milks me:	
	I would, while it was smiling in my face,	
	Have plucked my nipple from his boneless gums,	30
	And dashed the brains out, had I so sworn as you	
	Have done to this.	
Macbeth.	If we should fail?	
Lady Macbeth.	We fail?	
	But screw your courage to the sticking-place,	
	And we'll not fail. When Duncan is asleep—	
	Whereto the rather shall his day's hard journey	35
	Soundly invite him, his two chamberlains	

(Continued on page 101.)

(Continued from page 100.)

> Will I with wine and wassail so convince,
> That memory, the <u>warder</u> of the brain,
> Shall be a fume, and the receipt of reason
> A limbeck only: when in swinish sleep   40
> Their drenchèd natures lie, as in a death,
> What cannot you and I perform upon
> Th' unguarded Duncan? What not put upon
> His spongy officers, who shall bear the guilt
> Of our great quell?

Macbeth.   Bring forth men-children only;   45
> For thy <u>undaunted</u> mettle should compose
> Nothing but males. Will it not be received,
> When we have marked with blood those sleepy two
> Of his own chamber, and used their very daggers,
> That they have done't?

Lady Macbeth.   Who dares receive it other,   50
> As we shall make our griefs and clamor roar
> Upon his death?

Macbeth.   I am settled, and bend up
> Each corporal agent to this terrible feat.
> Away, and mock the time with fairest show:
> False face must hide what the false heart doth know.   55
>
>   *Exeunt*

Understanding Vocabulary *(20 points)*

Each underlined word below has also been underlined in the excerpt from *Macbeth*. Re-read those passages, and use context clues to help you select an answer. Write the letter of the word that *best* completes each sentence. *(4 points each)*

_____ **1.** To have <u>valor</u> is to have

     a. pride   **b.** fear   **c.** courage

_____ **2.** <u>Prithee</u> is a way of saying

     a. "you"   **b.** "please"   **c.** "listen"

_____ **3.** An <u>enterprise</u> is

     a. a plan   **b.** a promise   **c.** news

_____ **4.** A <u>warder</u> is a

     a. wife   **b.** guard   **c.** soldier

_____ **5.** Someone who is <u>undaunted</u> is

     a. tired   **b.** resolute   **c.** wholesome

Thoughtful Reading *(35 points)*

On the line provided, write the letter of the *best* answer to each of the following items. *(7 points each)*

_____ **6.** The major conflict in the passage is between

     a. Macbeth and Duncan   **c.** love and fear within Lady Macbeth
     b. youth and age   **d.** ambition and conscience within Macbeth

(Continued on page 102.)

*Drama Study Guide: **The Tragedy of Julius Caesar***

(Continued from page 101.)

_____ **7.** The reader knows the conflict is resolved when

    a. Macbeth says, "If we should fail?"
    b. Macbeth says, "I am settled. . . ."
    c. Macbeth says, "Bring forth men-children only. . . ."
    d. Lady Macbeth says, "Screw your courage to the sticking-place. . . ."

_____ **8.** In this passage, Macbeth is mobilized to act by his

    a. deep hatred of Duncan
    b. patriotism
    c. wife's ambitious taunting
    d. fear of detection

_____ **9.** Lady Macbeth uses the horrifying image of killing a child to show that she

    a. does not love her children
    b. is not afraid
    c. loves her husband
    d. keeps her promises

_____ **10.** Who does Macbeth think will be blamed for Duncan's death?

    a. himself
    b. the guards
    c. his wife
    d. Duncan himself

Expanded Response *(15 points)*

11. Which word below do you think *best* characterizes Lady Macbeth? On the lines provided, write the letter of the answer you choose, and briefly defend your choice. There is more than one possible answer. Use at least one example from the excerpt to support your ideas.

    a. courageous   **b.** determined   **c.** honorable   **d.** ambitious

_____

_____

_____

_____

_____

_____

_____

Written Response *(30 points)*

12. Macbeth, like Brutus in *The Tragedy of Julius Caesar,* is considered a tragic hero. On a separate sheet of paper, write a paragraph that compares and contrasts Macbeth and Brutus, specifically exploring their motives for murder and their misgivings. (Macbeth is ultimately killed for slaying Duncan.) Use at least two examples from each play to support your ideas.

*Drama Study Guide: **The Tragedy of Julius Caesar***

Staging the Play

When you've finished reading *The Tragedy of Julius Caesar,* plan to perform scenes from the play. Here are some suggestions.

Getting Started

1. Form **acting groups.** Each group should select a director, set designer, actors, a prop manager, a costume designer, a sound-effects technician (thunder is important in some scenes), and a prompter. You might want to give your acting companies names.

2. Each acting group should select a different scene to perform.

3. Prepare **scripts** of your scene: one for each actor, one for the director, and one for the prompter. The scripts should be typed on 8½ × 11-inch sheets of paper, with extra space between the lines.

4. The **director** and **actors** should work together to write **character analyses** of each character in the scene. Focus on these questions: What does the character want? What are the character's feelings and motives at this point in the play? What is distinct about the character?

5. The **prop manager** must check the dialogue and stage directions carefully and supply all the physical properties needed by the actors: candles, torches, spears, letters, and so on.

6. The **set designer** should sketch the set and perhaps make a shoe-box model. When you are rehearsing, be sure you know where actors are to stand, how they should move around onstage, and where they should enter and exit.

> *Without wonder and insight, acting is just a trade. With it, it becomes creation.*
>
> —Bette Davis

> *I can never remember being afraid of an audience. If the audience could do better, they'd be up here onstage and I'd be out there watching them.*
>
> —Ethel Merman

Rehearsals

As they rehearse, actors and directors should indicate on their scripts when characters should pause, what words should be stressed, what gestures should be used. Actors might also want to note words that give them trouble. They might also note what their character is feeling.

To overcome any "fear" of poetry, rewrite the lines in your scripts so they don't look like poetry. Don't change any words; just write the lines as prose. Go back to Act I, Scene 2, lines 190–198, and reread the conversation between Caesar and Antony. Then, look at it here, written as prose:

Caesar. Antonius.

Antony. Caesar?

Caesar. Let me have men about me that are fat, sleek-headed men, and such as sleep a-nights. Yond Cassius has a lean and hungry look; he thinks too much: such men are dangerous.

Antony. Fear him not, Caesar, he's not dangerous; he is a noble Roman, and well given.

Caesar. Would he were fatter! But I fear him not.

With a partner, read both versions aloud. Which version seems easier to read?

> *Every now and then, when you're on the stage, you hear the best sound a player can hear. It is a sound you can't get in movies or in television. It is the sound of a wonderful, deep silence that means you've hit them where they live.*
>
> —Shelley Winters

(Continued on page 104.)

Drama Study Guide: The Tragedy of Julius Caesar

HRW MATERIAL COPYRIGHTED UNDER NOTICE APPEARING EARLIER IN THIS WORK.

103

(Continued from page 103.)

Finding a Scene

Choose a scene that you think you would *enjoy playing*. Here are some suggestions:

- Act I, Scene 2: large cast; big speeches for Cassius
- Act II, Scene 1: large cast; big speeches for Brutus
- Act II, Scene 2: special effects—thunder and lightning
- Act II, Scene 4: small cast; important scene for Portia
- Act III, Scene 1: the assassination; large cast; complex stage movement
- Act III, Scene 2: the great funeral orations; exciting acting opportunity

Cross-Curricular Activity

Humanities

Assignment

Have you ever noticed how background music can affect the mood of a movie or a television show? Although we are sometimes not consciously aware of this music, it can make the action on the screen seem more dramatic, more romantic, more violent, more peaceful, or more suspenseful.

Even a sunset over an ocean can seem foreboding with certain music playing in the background. A chase scene can seem frightening or hilarious, depending not only on the action but also on the mood set by the background music.

Shakespeare's carefully chosen words describe the action in *The Tragedy of Julius Caesar* in images that are memorable, even without background music. For this assignment, however, you will imagine the music Shakespeare would have played had he been given the musical choices we have today. With a partner you will choose a scene from the play and select a piece of music that complements the scene's mood and action.

Equipment

- Audio equipment (a cassette, CD, or record player)

Selecting a Scene and Music

With your partner, review several scenes of the play. Select three or four that you like, and identify the reasons why you like them. Consider, for example, the sense of foreboding in the soothsayer's warning, the drama of the storm as Cassius plans Caesar's murder, Portia's tender plea for Brutus to confide in her, the brutal murder, Antony's inspiring funeral oration, or Cassius's despair as he faces death.

Read aloud the three or four scenes you have selected, and choose the one that appeals the most to you and your partner. Then, discuss the scene's setting, action, characters, and mood. Brainstorm to find words that describe the scene or characters, such as *thoughtful, inspiring, eerie, brooding, angry, triumphant, worried,* or *sorrowful.*

Then, consider the kinds of music that might best complement the scene you have chosen. You might check your school or community library for recordings that can be borrowed. Experiment with different types of music, from classical to popular, before making your final choice. Do *not* select music that might offend even one person in the class.

As you are exploring different pieces of music, you might listen to selections by Giuseppe Verdi, an Italian composer who loved Shakespeare's plays. Verdi was inspired by Shakespeare's plays to write several operas (with the apparent exception of *The Tragedy of Julius Caesar*).

Sharing What You Learned

You and your partner will read your scene aloud for the class while your music selection plays. Be prepared to explain why you chose that piece of music. Invite classmates' opinions on the appropriateness of your choice.

After the presentations, discuss these questions as a class:

- If two groups chose the same scene but different music, what were the differences and similarities in their musical choices?
- How could markedly different pieces of music be appropriate for the same scene?
- Do you think *The Tragedy of Julius Caesar* would be improved by playing background music as you read it?

Peer/Self-Evaluation

When evaluating your work for this project, consider these points:

- In what ways did your musical selection reinforce the mood, setting, or action in the scene you chose?
- In what ways, if any, did your music detract from the scene?
- How clearly did you explain to the class the reasons for your selection?

(Continued on page 106.)

(Continued from page 105.)

Other Ideas for Cross-Curricular Activities

Students could work individually or together to prepare presentations on the following topics: the conflict and struggle between Queen Elizabeth and Mary Queen of Scots; Elizabethan theories of astrology; the activities at Roman public festivals (such as the feast of Lupercal); or Roman religious beliefs and ceremonies. Encourage students to be creative in their reports, using illustrations, diagrams, and dramatic reenactments.

Students would also enjoy, and learn from, a forum of actors and directors. If your community or a local college has a theater group, invite members who have performed Shakespeare's plays to discuss their experiences and perhaps read a scene from *Julius Caesar*. Students should have many questions to ask concerning the difficulties (and pleasures) of Shakespeare's verse, the blocking of scenes in a modern theater, the process of re-creating or inventing gestures when the plays provide no direction, the arguments for and against modern-English and modern-dress productions, the actors' approaches to soliloquies, and so on.

Read On

Profiles in Courage by John F. Kennedy

Here John F. Kennedy provides portraits of some politicians who made courageous choices in difficult times. *Profiles in Courage* details the physical, political, and moral courage of such men as John Quincy Adams, Sam Houston, and Thomas Hart Benton. Find out how much strength, courage, and conviction are needed when human beings are struggling to hold a country together.

The Tragedy of Macbeth
by William Shakespeare

Julius Caesar is not the only Shakespearean tragedy about a political assassination. In 1040, a Scottish chieftain named Macbeth defeated and killed King Duncan I and seized the throne of Scotland. Shakespeare dramatized this story in his tragedy *Macbeth*. Macbeth is quick to sacrifice his honor for the sake of ambition, so you may find that this tale of intrigue in ancient Scotland provides some shocking contrasts to the issues raised in *The Tragedy of Julius Caesar*.

The Right Stuff by Tom Wolfe

What makes people decide to become astronauts? What qualifications must a person have to become an astronaut? How quickly can someone become a hero, and how quickly can the public forget all about that hero? In Tom Wolfe's cliffhanger *The Right Stuff,* you'll find an intriguing treatment of these and other issues relating to the early years of America's space exploration.

The Lion in Winter directed by
Anthony Harvey

Life was pretty risky in England and France during the time of Henry II and Eleanor of Aquitaine. *The Lion in Winter,* Anthony Harvey's 1968 movie about medieval royal problems, features Henry and Eleanor, who married in 1152 and proceeded to fight bitterly about their kingdoms. Ambition is rampant in their household. Honor is harder to find.

Animal Farm by George Orwell

When the farm animals revolt, the farmer's long reign is over. George Orwell's *Animal Farm* is the tale of a barnyard menagerie that becomes a mirror of human society. The big question: Will the animals form the perfect society, or will another tyrant take over and terrorize the farm?

The Day They Shot Lincoln by Jim Bishop

Jim Bishop's careful retelling of a shocking assassination, *The Day They Shot Lincoln,* chronicles a single day in the history of the United States, a day that changed the country forever. More than the story of a murder, Bishop's book is a powerful portrait of a nation—its leaders and its citizens, its past and its future.

The Power and the Glory by Graham Greene

The flawed protagonist of Graham Greene's *The Power and the Glory* is a priest who is being hunted down by an unfair government. Greene portrays the priest as a man who in the end is able to stand up for something he believes in.

"Harrison Bergeron" by Kurt Vonnegut

What if everything you did was controlled by the government? What if everyone was exactly like everybody else? What if computers could read minds? These are the questions Kurt Vonnegut explores in "Harrison Bergeron," his classic science fiction tale—about a society in chains and a young hero who tries to save the people from mindless tyranny.

Antigone by Jean Anouilh

First produced in 1942, when the Nazis were occupying France, Jean Anouilh's daring adaptation of Sophocles' *Antigone* was censored by the collaborationist government—because it dared to question authority. Anouilh uses this ancient tragedy to ask some hard questions about life and politics in the twentieth century.

JFK directed by Oliver Stone

Oliver Stone's version of the John F. Kennedy assassination—depicted in his 1991 film *JFK*—has stirred up some controversial questions: Who really shot John Kennedy? Was a conspiracy involved? What about that second gunman?

Drama Study Guide: The Tragedy of Julius Caesar

HRW MATERIAL COPYRIGHTED UNDER NOTICE APPEARING EARLIER IN THIS WORK.

107

Answer Key

Graphic Organizer for Active Reading, Act I

Responses will vary. Sample responses follow.

Graphic Organizer

Marullus: Scene 1, lines 32–37 or 50–51
Summary: Caesar is a conqueror who brings nothing home to Rome.

Flavius: Scene 1, lines 72–75
Summary: Caesar is a high-flying bird whose feathers need to be plucked.

Brutus: Scene 2, lines 79–80
Summary: Caesar is a potential king.

Casca: Scene 2, lines 234–240
Summary: Caesar is an insincere leader who manipulates the emotions of people in order to gain power.

Cassius: Scene 2, lines 111–131, 135–138, or 149–150
Summary: Caesar is a giant statue towering over fearful men.

1. *Cassius:* Scene 2, lines 140–150. Predator imagery portrays Caesar growing fat from feeding off the bodies of others. The overall effect is to make Caesar appear to be an ambitious opportunist who is using others.

2. Brutus's portrayal of Caesar as a man who is eager and likely to become king is most believable, since it seems to be based on a reasonable, rather than an emotional, view of Caesar's character and past actions.

Making Meanings, Act I

Reviewing the Text

a. The workers are celebrating the feast of Lupercal and Caesar's return to Rome after defeating Pompey's sons. Marullus rebukes them for ignoring their debt of gratitude to Pompey, their former hero, and for supporting Caesar.

b. The soothsayer warns Caesar, "Beware the ides of March" (March 15), but Caesar ignores him.

c. According to Casca, Caesar turned down all three offers of the crown. Caesar made a show of offering the crowd his life but then fainted.

d. Caesar is deaf in one ear and epileptic.

e. Cassius asks Cinna to place letters supposedly written by other citizens in Brutus's house and on the statue of Brutus's ancestor.

f. Cicero and Casca discuss the supernatural events that happen on a stormy night in Rome. They are disturbed that these events might foreshadow Caesar's tyranny.

g. Cassius instructs Cinna to place throughout Brutus's house forged letters that urge Brutus to oppose Caesar.

First Thoughts

1. Students may name contemporary monarchs and dictators whose governments should provide a variety of political structures for comparison and contrast.

Shaping Interpretations

2. The violent storm—with its thunder, lightning, and eerie "fire"—is both dangerous and foreboding. Shakespeare also uses reports of supernatural phenomena—burning men, a lion at the Capitol, an owl shrieking at noon, groups of terrified women, open graves, ghosts—to build a sinister mood.

3. Cassius seems cunning, persuasive, and deceitful. By the end of the act, he has persuaded Brutus to consider the plot, recruited Casca, forged letters to Brutus, and called a meeting of the conspirators.

4. Some Romans believe that Caesar is a strong, effective leader who should be crowned king. Others believe that he is a tyrant who threatens the republic and should be deposed.

5. In the first line of the play, Flavius describes the commoners as "idle creatures"; later in the scene (lines 35–55), Marullus rails against their ingratitude and fickleness. In Scene 2, Casca's speeches are filled with venomous descriptions of the people. In Scene 3, Cassius characterizes the populace as "womanish" (lines 80–84) and as servile garbage (lines 103–111).

6. Brutus's extensive dialogue with Cassius in the second scene of this act reveals him to have positive and negative character traits. Perhaps Brutus's most admirable qualities are his selflessness and idealism. Brutus is genuinely concerned with the welfare of the Roman populace. On the other hand, Brutus's weaknesses are his gullibility and irrationality. In this act, Brutus seems to be rapidly falling for Cassius's

Drama Study Guide: The Tragedy of Julius Caesar

108

HRW MATERIAL COPYRIGHTED UNDER NOTICE APPEARING EARLIER IN THIS WORK.

arguments against Caesar, arguments that appeal largely to emotion and contain very little concrete evidence.

7. Caesar is revered by the populace and by some senators as a strong, successful leader—a man of decisive action. He is accessible to the masses, and he is a keen judge of character. From another viewpoint, Caesar is impetuous, power hungry, vain, and calculating.

Extending the Text

8. *Evaluation.* Encourage students to explain their choices. The following are just a few sample responses:
   - "When Caesar says 'Do this,' it is performed." (Scene 2, line 10)
   - "The fault, dear Brutus, is not in our stars, / But in ourselves. . . ." (Scene 2, lines 140–141)
   - "For who so firm that cannot be seduced?" (Scene 2, line 310)
   - "So every bondman in his own hand bears / The power to cancel his captivity." (Scene 3, lines 101–102)

9. *Synthesis.* The Roman commoners are easily swayed and shift loyalties according to the moment; thus, they are susceptible to colorful, theatrical leaders. Students may suggest that any large crowd—in ancient Rome or today—can act irrationally and on the inspiration of the moment.

Choices: Building Your Portfolio, Act I

Performance

After partners have determined the characters of Cassius and Brutus, ask them to choose several sections of dialogue that reveal their characteristics.

Vocabulary Mini-Lesson, Act I

Try It Out

Responses will vary. Pun maps created by students should either indicate the dual meaning of a single word or point out the homophonic relationship between two different words. Examples: *lie*—"an untruth" or "to put oneself in a reclining position"; *son*—"the male offspring of a man and a woman" or *sun*—"the star that provides light and heat for the Earth."

Words to Own Worksheet, Act I

Developing Vocabulary

Sentences will vary. Sample responses follow. Vocabulary words are shown in italics.

1. Mark Chapman plotted without *conspirators* to kill John Lennon.
2. The occupation of *soothsayer* is not as common today as it was during the Middle Ages.
3. After the successful concert, the singer was *exalted* by her fans.
4. The *servile* role of women is considered acceptable in some cultures.
5. The *barren* landscape provided a welcome respite from the city clutter.
6. Students loved Mr. Garza not only because he was a good teacher but also because of his pleasant *countenance*.
7. The actor proclaimed dramatically, "For *aught* I know, my mind is gone."
8. The house was washed away in a raging *torrent* during the rainstorm and flood.
9. The *blunt* truth is sometimes difficult medicine to swallow.
10. The *portentous* sky forewarned a dramatic storm.

Language Link Worksheet, Act I

Exercise A

1. complement	6. accept, counsel
2. accept, except	7. principal, complement
3. allusion	8. advises
4. infer	9. advise
5. affects	10. counsel

Exercise B

Corrections are shown in italics.

Are Caesar's ambition and power *illusions*? In Act I, Cassius argues that Caesar is *affected* by his power and will inevitably become a tyrant. It is a *compliment* to Shakespeare's skill as a writer to say that Cassius's *principal* motivation at the beginning of the play is not entirely obvious. Can we *infer* from Cassius's words that he is jealous of Caesar's growing power? Or should we accept Cassius's words at face value? Since the storm at the end of the act is an *allusion* to the storm that will soon erupt in the Roman state, we know that

Drama Study Guide: The Tragedy of Julius Caesar

HRW MATERIAL COPYRIGHTED UNDER NOTICE APPEARING EARLIER IN THIS WORK.

109

whatever Cassius's motives, the effects of his actions will not be peaceful. Cassius is skilled at complimenting others in order to persuade them to join his *council.* Soon, despite the advice of the soothsayer, Caesar will walk into the storm created by Cassius. Whatever we may infer from Cassius's motives, we must consider that he is concerned with the *principle* of freedom, whether it be for himself or for others.

Literary Elements Worksheet, Act I

Understanding Setting

1. b	6. d
2. a	7. f
3. a	8. f
4. d	9. e
5. c	

Applying Skills

1. flowers
2. cloak
3. dagger
4. paper

Reader's Response

Responses will vary. The most likely responses are *foreboding, hint of evil, confusion,* and *mystery.*

Test, Act I

Thoughtful Reading

1. b   2. c   3. a   4. d   5. d

Expanded Response

6. Responses will vary. Students should use at least one example from the selection to support their ideas. The best answers are **b** and **c**. Guidelines for evaluating responses to each choice follow.

   a. Partial credit may be given. While honor is spoken of with some frequency, and the characters all wish be to considered honorable, none of the characters, with the possible exception of Brutus, seems motivated by a personal code of ethical behavior.

   b. Students should recognize that it is the fear of the potential tyranny of Caesar that drives the other characters to plan his downfall.

   c. Students may infer that Cassius is envious of Caesar's growing power and popularity and that Cassius is a man who cannot stand for others to have more than he has.

   d. Partial credit may be given. Students may note that flattery is used by Cassius to lure Brutus into the conspiracy, but it has no other major role in this act.

7. Responses may vary but should be reasonable examples of what could be foreshadowed by the content of the quotations. Sample responses follow.
   • This quotation might foreshadow Brutus's choosing death by his own hand rather than losing his honor. Brutus prefers to kill himself and preserve his honor and reputation.
   • This quotation might foreshadow Cassius's death at his own hand.
   • This quotation might foreshadow an encounter between Brutus and death.

Written Response

8. Responses will vary. In a model response, students should fulfill the following criteria:
   • demonstrate understanding of the prompt
   • clearly describe how Cassius's view of the storm's meaning differs from Cicero's view and offer a reasonable alternative interpretation of the storm
   • support their ideas with at least two examples from the play. For example:
     • Cassius sees the storm as a call to end Caesar's tyranny. It is the gods' harsh commentary on Caesar's growing ambition and a warning that a horrible disaster will descend if Caesar isn't stopped.
     • Cassius's plan to destroy Caesar is the eruption that will upset the order of the state.

Graphic Organizer for Active Reading, Act II

Responses will vary. Sample responses follow.

Graphic Organizer

Brutus's Actions: "I have not slept." (Scene 1, line 62)

Brutus's Words: "Let's be sacrificers, but not butchers. . . ." (Scene 1, line 166)

Others' Actions: Portia—"I have made strong proof of my constancy, / Giving myself a volun-

Drama Study Guide: The Tragedy of Julius Caesar

110

HRW MATERIAL COPYRIGHTED UNDER NOTICE APPEARING EARLIER IN THIS WORK.

tary wound / Here in the thigh. . . ." (Scene 1, lines 299–301)

Others' Words: Portia—"Brutus is wise. . . ." (Scene 1, line 258)

Ligarius—"I am not sick, if Brutus have in hand / Any exploit worthy the name of honor." (Scene 1, lines 316–317)

1. Brutus's soliloquy shows that he does not trust Caesar to restrain his love of power in the future. It also suggests that Brutus needs sound reasons in order to act violently; he does not act solely on emotion or from personal motives.

2. Brutus is the hero so far because he is more interested in the welfare of the state than in personal gain, in contrast with Caesar and Cassius, who are motivated by personal gain and envy. Caesar seems to be the villain at this point because he is vain and self-deluded.

Making Meanings, Act II

Reviewing the Text

a. Brutus claims that he is acting for the public good, that kingship could turn Caesar's natural inclinations—ambition and love of power—into tyranny, and that once crowned, Caesar would ignore those below him.

b. Cassius proposes the murder. Brutus argues that Antony's murder could seem unnecessarily vicious and could turn public sentiment against the conspirators.

c. Portia demands to know what is troubling Brutus and who has visited him in such secrecy.

d. Calphurnia urges Caesar to avoid going to the Senate meeting by pretending that he is ill. Calphurnia does this because she had a nightmare in which a statue of Caesar bled into the streets and the Romans bathed their hands in his blood.

e. Decius spontaneously reinterprets Calphurnia's dream to mean that Caesar's blood is the lifeblood of the Roman Empire. Decius also tells Caesar that the Senate is going to offer Caesar a crown that day.

f. Portia is afraid that someone will tell Caesar about the conspiracy against him. She is deeply concerned about Brutus's welfare.

First Thoughts

1. Responses will vary. Sample response: Brutus and Cassius have chosen one evil (murder) in the hope of preventing another (tyranny). As absolute moral choices, Brutus and Cassius cite the general good, the republic (an ideal that encompasses equality, freedom, and justice), and honor.

Shaping Interpretations

2. Responses will vary. Sample response: The pace of Act II is slower than the pace of Act I and the characters more agitated. In Scene 1, Brutus and the other conspirators spend a sleepless and agonizing night waiting for the fateful day. Brutus's wife, Portia, cannot sleep. In Scene 2, Caesar says that his wife, Calphurnia, has spent a restless night. In Scene 3, Artemidorus waits to warn Caesar of the conspiracy. In Scene 4, Portia waits to hear of the results of her husband's plot. Act II is thus dominated by fearful waiting.

3. Responses will vary. Sample response: Brutus says that the need for an oath shows weakness in those who take the oath or in the cause that they support. This speech indicates that Brutus is an honorable, patriotic, and trusting Roman.

4. Responses will vary. Sample response: Caesar is confident yet indecisive, fearful yet determined to conquer his fear, superstitious yet wise in accepting what he cannot change, and arrogant yet trusting. Although Caesar is no monster; many will have little sympathy for him.

5. At the end of Scene 1, the thunder underscores the momentousness of the conspirators' action; it concludes the scene on a note of passion. At the beginning of Scene 2, the thunder creates a sense of danger and foreboding. The characters interpret the heavens' disturbance in conflicting ways, as evidence of a present evil (Caesar's rule) and as a portent of a coming evil (his assassination).

Connecting with the Text

6. In each scene, Shakespeare introduces a character (Artemidorus and the soothsayer, respectively) whose warnings could still prevent the assassination.

7. Responses will vary. Many will feel that Brutus's argument is weak. He has no specific evidence to indicate that Caesar would be a harmful leader; rather, he bases his argument on the assumption that power will corrupt Caesar. Perhaps Brutus should allow Caesar to take power but observe him closely, working in the meantime to gather greater support in the Senate. Then, if Caesar's behavior becomes intolerable, Brutus can work with the Senate to put Caesar out of power.

Drama Study Guide: The Tragedy of Julius Caesar

HRW MATERIAL COPYRIGHTED UNDER NOTICE APPEARING EARLIER IN THIS WORK.

111

Extending the Text

8. *Evaluation and Synthesis:* Responses will vary. Some may feel that the omission is not a major problem; others may be bothered that Shakespeare has left them to figure out this detail on their own. If students believe that Portia opposes Brutus's participation in the conspiracy, then they might write a scene in which Portia passionately pleads with her husband to get away from the conspirators. If students believe that Portia supports her husband, then they might have her urge him to be very careful.

9. *Evaluation:* Responses will vary. Looking at the issue from today's standpoint, students will probably disagree with Portia's self-assessment. Encourage them to give factual reasons for their responses.

Choices: Building Your Portfolio, Act II

Performance

Students' preparation should show an understanding of character motivation.

Vocabulary Mini-Lesson, Act II

Try It Out

Responses will vary. Sample responses follow.

1. I cannot guess how close to sunrise it is.

2. *good* or *welfare*

3. Lucius means that they have pulled their hats low on their heads, to hide their faces.

4. *path,* meaning "walk"

Words to Own Worksheet, Act II

Developing Vocabulary

Sentences will vary. Sample responses follow. Vocabulary words are shown in italics.

1. Every *taper* in Mother's house was lighted at dusk.

2. The princess resolved to *spurn* all offers of courtship, in anticipation of Prince Charming.

3. Managers cannot rely on *base* personnel to save a business from financial failure.

4. *Augmented* by the deck, the house has increased significantly in value.

5. To *redress* the accident, the insurance company agreed to pay the claimant ten thousand dollars.

6. Anger at the university president's insensitivity sparked a student *insurrection.*

7. The kindest *visage* is a smiling one.

8. Tonya's *affability* won her the lead role in the school play.

9. The married couple's *constancy* was evident in their love for each other.

10. The approaching tornado signaled that danger was *imminent.*

Language Link Worksheet, Act II

Understanding Shakespeare's Language

Responses may vary. Sample responses follow.

1. figure

2. The adjective *weak* follows, rather than precedes, the noun *motives.*

3. away from here

4. sound him out

5. *other;* Shall no other man but only Caesar be touched?

6. *to be*

7. *to expose*

8. have met with you; have had access to you

9. Do you plan to go out?

10. *go*

11. *purpose;* Whose end is planned by the mighty gods?

12. keeps; Calphurnia, my wife, is making me stay home.

13. keep an eye on

14. get close to; make requests of

15. What time is it?

Literary Elements Worksheet, Act II

Understanding Characterization

1. b	**3.** a
2. a	**4.** b

Applying Skills

1. Brutus has a conscience; it's not easy for him to agree to kill anyone, even a dictator.

Drama Study Guide: ***The Tragedy of Julius Caesar***

2. Brutus is tremendously respected by other Romans.

3. Brutus is a good enough man to inspire love in a strong woman.

Test, Act II

Thoughtful Reading

1. a   2. d   3. c   4. a   5. c

Expanded Response

6. Responses will vary. Students should use at least one example from the selection to support their ideas. The best answers are **b** and **c**. Guidelines for evaluating responses to each choice follow.

   a. Partial credit might be given. Students might argue that because both wives eventually go along with what their husbands wants, they are submissive. However, they both show stronger mettle than a truly submissive wife would. Portia stabs herself in the thigh, and Calphurnia at first succeeds in persuading Caesar to stay home.

   b. Students might recognize that both wives are devoted to their husbands and that their disagreements are based on a concern for their husbands' well-being.

   c. Students might recognize that both wives are self-sacrificing in that they put their husbands' interests before their own. Calphurnia allows Caesar to use her as a reason for not going to the Senate; she would rather appear domineering than allow her husband to be killed. Portia's selflessness is shown when she stabs herself to demonstrate her loyalty.

   d. Partial credit might be given. Though this is not a supportable response, some students might argue that the wives want their husbands around for selfish reasons—so that they won't be alone.

7. Responses will vary. Sample responses follow.

Question: Will Brutus tell Portia about the conspiracy?

Answer: It appears that he does tell her, given her lines at the end of the scene, though we do not see him do so.

Question: Will Caesar stay home?

Answer: He decides to stay home, then is persuaded to go.

Question: Will Artemidorus get Caesar to read his letter?

Answer: No; Caesar is too arrogant to heed any warnings.

Question: Will Caesar be killed?

Answer: Yes; because of his overconfidence and lack of suspicion.

Question: How will Antony respond to Caesar's death?

Answer: He will kill himself, join with Brutus, or form a faction against Brutus.

Written Response

8. Responses will vary. In a model response, students should fulfill the following criteria:

   • demonstrate understanding of the prompt

   • clearly explain how the lines reflect both Brutus's inner conflict and the play's outer conflict

   • support their ideas with at least two specific examples from the play. For example:

     • Brutus is physically unwell and unable to sleep at the beginning of the act due to his inner turmoil over whether to kill Caesar. He is caught in a waking nightmare.

     • In the same way there is turmoil in the heavens as the faction makes plans to upset civil order.

     • The insurrection will culminate with Caesar's murder followed by civil unrest.

Graphic Organizer for Active Reading, Act III

Responses will vary. Sample responses and guidelines for evaluating responses follow.

Graphic Organizer

Before Act III: Act I, Scene 2, lines 9–10, 28–29, 234–235; Act II, Scene 1, lines 155–161, 165, 181–184; Scene 2, lines 52–53

In Act III: Scene 1, lines 138–139, 173–176, 191–203, 224–230, 254–255; Scene 2, lines 66, 118, 218–224

Summaries should convey that Antony appears to be Caesar's happy-go-lucky right-hand man in the first two acts. In the third act, he shows himself as clever, loyal, and manipulative.

1. Students should recognize that Antony becomes the driving force in Act III. Some will admire his loyalty to and affection for Caesar and see him as genuinely horrified by the violence of the assassination. Others will see him

Drama Study Guide: The Tragedy of Julius Caesar

HRW MATERIAL COPYRIGHTED UNDER NOTICE APPEARING EARLIER IN THIS WORK.

113

as an underhanded opportunist, vengeful and manipulative.

2. Students' predictions should be based on the action of the play so far and the way in which the Roman populace and leadership have been portrayed.

Making Meanings, Act III

Reviewing the Text

a. Decius intervenes with another suit, and Artemidorus inadvertently offers the wrong argument for having his suit read first. He specifies its personal importance to Caesar, prompting Caesar to make a show of hearing it last.

b. Metellus Cimber asks Caesar to repeal the banishment of his brother, Publius Cimber.

c. Cassius fears that Antony will turn the people against the conspirators. Responding, Brutus says that he will explain the killing before Antony speaks and will make clear that the conspirators want Antony to honor Caesar.

d. Antony becomes the protagonist as he pledges a civil war to avenge Caesar and destroy the assassins. Students may find the preparation in the fact that Cassius warned that Antony's great love for Caesar could make him a formidable enemy.

e. Antony announces that Caesar has bequeathed to each citizen seventy-five drachmas along with his private arbors and orchards on one side of the Tiber. The crowd responds by rushing out to hunt down the conspirators.

f. They kill a poet by the name of Cinna because they mistake him for the conspirator of the same name.

First Thoughts

1. Responses will vary. Some students may identify more with Antony's speech. They may feel that Brutus has overreacted to his own fear about what Caesar may have become. Other students may identify with Brutus's speech because they believe that Caesar could have become a dangerous tyrant.

Shaping Interpretations

2. Antony vows that the assassins will pay for the murder with their lives. The speech seems to foreshadow a great conflict—perhaps even a civil war—in which that payment will be made.

3. Antony presents Caesar's good qualities and achievements as facts but always adds, in effect, "However, Brutus says otherwise." Thus he does not directly oppose Brutus, but he does present opposing evidence: Caesar was a faithful friend; Caesar filled Rome's coffers; Caesar wept with the poor; Caesar refused the crown. "Honorable" men, Antony implies, would not kill such a man.

4. According to Brutus, Antony is given "to sports, to wildness, and much company" and lacks Caesar's intelligence, drive, and power. Caesar delights in Antony's carousing but also values his opinions. Only Cassius sees Antony as shrewd, devious, dangerously loyal to Caesar, and in a position of power. Students should give their reasons for why they do or do not agree.

5. Shakespeare indicates that the mob is bloodthirsty and irrational. The people want to act—destructively—not think.

6. Brutus's decision marks the turning point. The assassins have the possibility of securing public support for their act, but Antony usurps the people's allegiance. Students may predict that the conspirators will flee Rome.

7. The lines also can mean that others will repeat the assassins' actions—that other people will overthrow tyranny in the name of liberty.

Connecting with the Text

8. Students should note that both Brutus and Antony seem to desire to influence the Roman crowd. Students may say that they see this same behavior in politicians today.

Choices: Building Your Portfolio, Act III

Creative Writing

Students' scenes should attempt to capture the shoemaker's irreverent humor.

Words to Own Worksheet, Act III

Developing Vocabulary

Sentences will vary. Sample responses follow. Vocabulary words are shown in italics.

1. Orange blazed across the evening *firmament*.

2. Chin made a *valiant* effort to rescue the tiny kitten in the oak tree.

3. Georgia's mom asked her to *fetch* the remote control.

Drama Study Guide: **The Tragedy of Julius Caesar**

4. I *beseech* you to follow the plan carefully.

5. The *plebeians* provided the empire with necessary services.

6. Who can *censure* the dedicated teacher for her students' failing grades?

7. Freshly shoveled earth in the yard marks where the family dog was *interred.*

8. The millionaire is *bequeathing* his estate to the community.

9. The king's *legacy* remains for his sons.

10. The skilled *orator* moved the crowd to mutiny.

Literary Elements Worksheet, Act III

Responses will vary. Sample responses follow.

Understanding Imagery

1. **a.** blood, elbows, swords, market place, red weapons

   b. stoop, bathe, besmear, walk, waving

   c. sickened

2. **a.** purpled

   b. reek, smoke

Applying Skills

1. **a.** eyes; the blood is flowing as freely as tears.

   b. weeping is associated with sadness and death, especially violent death.

2. **a.** mouths; of their shape and red edges, which resemble lips

   b. mouths speak, and these wounds beg Antony to speak on Caesar's behalf.

Test, Act III

Thoughtful Reading

1. d   **2.** b   **3** c   **4** a   **5.** b

Expanded Response

6. Responses will vary. Students should use at least one example from the play to support their ideas. The best answers are **a, b,** and **c.** Guidelines for evaluating responses to each choice follow.

   a. Students might recognize that unlike Cassius, Brutus is unable to see people's hid-

den motivations. Brutus is overly trusting and innocent in the struggle for power.

   b. Students might argue that Brutus holds certain idealistic standards of honor for himself and others that keep him from seeing things as they really are.

   c. Students might recognize that Brutus justly wishes to allow Caesar's good points to be honored by Antony while he will make the compelling case for Caesar's assassination.

   d. Partial credit might be given. Brutus tells Cassius that Antony's speech will work in their favor—he wants desperately for their actions to be seen as honorable, and he thinks that allowing a speech in praise of Caesar will demonstrate their honorable motives. However, it seems out of character for Brutus to be scheming.

7. Responses will vary. Sample responses follow.

   Purposes: to foreshadow the deaths of the conspirators; to emphasize how a mob can be driven to such an emotional pitch that it will kill anyone for little or no reason; to point out the power of words—in this case the power of "bad verses"—the overt reason the mob gives for killing Cinna; to emphasize the power of Antony's words to drive the crowd into a frenzy

Written Response

8. Responses will vary. In a model response, students should fulfill the following criteria:
   - demonstrate understanding of the prompt
   - clearly describe the ways in which Antony turns the crowd into a mob of rioters
   - support their ideas with at least three specific examples from the play. For example:
     • Antony repeats the phrase "Brutus is an honorable man" until it appears ridiculous in contrast with the nobility of the slain Caesar.
     • Antony teases the crowd with Caesar's will, appealing to their curiosity and self-interest.
     • Antony breaks down emotionally before the crowd, which has the effect of showing him to be loyal and loving while Brutus, who has coolly delivered his speech, seems selfish, unfeeling, and calculating.
     • Antony holds up Caesar's torn cloak as a way of showing how excessively violent the murder was; Antony also treats the cloak as if it were Caesar himself.
     • Antony reads the will, using it to suggest what a good ruler Caesar was—making the crowd turn on the conspirators.

Drama Study Guide: The Tragedy of Julius Caesar

HRW MATERIAL COPYRIGHTED UNDER NOTICE APPEARING EARLIER IN THIS WORK.

115

Graphic Organizer for Active Reading, Act IV

Responses will vary. Sample responses follow.

Graphic Organizer

Physical Description: lean and hungry looking

Crimes: taking bribes, hoarding gold

Brief History: member of faction that killed Caesar; now general of army trying to oust the present government

Personality Traits: clever, cynical, ambitious, envious, scheming

Attitude Toward Government: People seek power to serve their own needs.

1. Brutus has forgiven Cassius and once again sees him as a noble friend.

2. Cassius always seemed a selfish and envious person who cared for no one but himself, but in Scene 3 he shows surprising concern for retaining Brutus's affection and respect.

Making Meanings, Act IV

Reviewing the Text

a. Brutus and Cassius, in exile, have raised armies to challenge the triumvirate. In turn, Octavius, Antony, and Lepidus are gathering a force to fight the conspirators.

b. They are deciding whom to sentence to death. Antony believes that Lepidus should be dropped from the triumvirate when his usefulness has run out. Octavius disagrees but says that he will not prevent Antony's action.

c. Brutus is beginning to doubt Cassius's honesty and loyalty.

d. Cassius is angry that Brutus, ignoring his appeals, publicly condemned Lucius Pella for taking bribes. Brutus has heard reports of Cassius's own bribe taking; he also is incensed at Cassius's refusal to send him gold to pay his soldiers.

e. Portia was lonely and depressed about the triumvirate's power. Brutus acknowledges his sorrow but will not dwell on it. He bears her death unemotionally.

f. Brutus sees the ghost of Caesar.

First Thoughts

1. Responses will vary. After seeing so much emotion and devotion from Antony in Act III,
many students will be surprised to see a meaner side of him here. Other students may point to a softened Cassius as a great surprise.

Shaping Interpretations

2. Antony is shown to be treacherous, dishonest, coldly calculating, and cruel. Some students may feel that the contrast is too extreme, the changes too abrupt. Others may disagree, pointing to earlier reports of Anthony's shallow selfishness.

3. Responses will vary. Students may suggest that the lights be set low, with perhaps a spotlight only on the action center stage. They may have armed soldiers standing in rows behind the action center stage.

4. Their anger vented, Brutus and Cassius reveal their strong feelings for each other. Brutus apologizes to Cassius for his "ill-tempered" words. For his part, Cassius says that he cannot bear Brutus's disapproval. By this scene's end, Brutus and Cassius have strengthened their friendship; furthermore, from this point on Cassius no longer schemes against Brutus.

5. In both meetings, the leaders are in conflict. Both Antony and Cassius reveal their greed and argue that they, as seasoned soldiers, know better the realities of war. Octavius and Brutus seem more principled and fair. Perhaps the major difference is that the conflict between Brutus and Cassius is far more emotional, yet their breach is more securely healed. On the other hand, although Octavius yields to Antony, his yielding only perpetuates disunity.

6. Brutus is familiar, kind, and solicitous. With Lucius his tenderness is fatherly. In all there is a peace revealed in this scene that will cease in the violence of battle.

7. If a real actor plays the ghost, the reality of the ghost's existence becomes more plausible. If a voice represents the ghost, the implication is that the ghost is a figment of Brutus's imagination. The ghost might represent Brutus's guilt or anguish.

Connecting with the Text

8. Responses will vary. Students will probably sympathize with either Brutus or Cassius rather than Antony. The two conspirators share a warm reconciliation after an argument in this act, whereas Antony demonstrates only ruthlessness.

9. Cassius seems to take Portia's death harder than Brutus does; his words in this passage are more heavily laced with emotion to show that

Cassius is an Epicurean. Brutus seems matter-of-fact about Portia's suicide to reflect the fact that he is a Stoic. Students should explain their feelings for Brutus and Cassius at this point in the play.

10. Responses will vary. Students should explain their choices—whether they are based on their personal sympathies or on their sense of which side will win the battle.

Choices: Building Your Portfolio, Act IV

Creative Writing/Speaking

Journal entries will vary.

Language Link Mini-Lesson, Act IV

Anachronisms

1. A *doublet,* or close-fitting jacket, was an Elizabethan garment rather than a Roman one.

2. A mechanical striking clock had not yet been invented.

3. Not until the second century A.D.—when parchment sheets were folded, sewn together, and protected with boards—did true books appear.

Try It Out

• Responses will vary. Sample responses: He could have replaced the anachronistic items with something appropriate for the time. For example:
  • *garment* or *toga* instead of *doublet*
  • a reference to the position of the moon in the night sky instead of the reference to the striking clock
  • *scroll* instead of *book*
• Responses will vary. Events from Act I that might lend themselves well to anachronism include the occupations of the workmen at the play's beginning or the circumstances under which Cassius had once saved Caesar from drowning.

Words to Own Worksheet, Act IV

Developing Vocabulary

Sentences will vary. Sample responses follow. Vocabulary words are shown in italics.

1. *Chastisement* from the principal was in order for the schoolchildren's inappropriate behavior toward the substitute teacher.

2. Engine oil improperly disposed of can *contaminate* a city's drinking water.

3. Pranksters love to *bait* unsuspecting victims.

4. A *choleric* person would be unsuited for a profession that requires patience.

5. *Covetous* onlookers gazed at the star's glamorous gown and jewels.

6. Thomas's decision to quit his job was unreasonable and *rash.*

7. Nimbleness is an indispensable quality for athletes and dancers alike.

8. To travel abroad without proper identification is a risky *venture.*

9. *Repose* after lunch is customary in some cultures.

10. Hotel guests claimed to have seen a similar *apparition* during the night.

Literary Elements Worksheet, Act IV

Understanding Conflict

1. d
2. c
3. a
4. b
5. d
6. a

Applying Skills

1. F
2. T
3. T
4. F
5. T
6. T
7. F
8. T
9. T
10. T
11. T

Reader's Response

Responses will vary.

Test, Act IV

Thoughtful Reading

1. b 2. a 3. d 4. c 5. a

Expanded Response

6. Responses will vary. Sample responses follow.

   a. *Moment*—the ghost's visit. *Placement of Actors*—soldiers sleeping on the stage in a haphazard arrangement as though they were lying down where they had been standing;

Drama Study Guide: The Tragedy of Julius Caesar

Brutus center stage; the ghost enters from the shadows just behind and to the right of Brutus. *Props*—weapons and soldiers' garb positioned around the stage to look like that of an army preparing for battle. *Lighting*—Lights fade and become amber; candles or lanterns are used to create darkness and shadows.

    b. *Moment*—Cassius draws his dagger. *Placement of Actors*—Brutus and Cassius in Brutus's tent, center stage. *Props*—a table; Brutus and Cassius dressed for battle, with daggers and swords. *Lighting*—dim, as though from lanterns or a fire, with the two men spotlighted so that all attention is focused on them.

7. Responses will vary. Students should use at least one example from the play to support their ideas. The best answers are **a, b,** and **d.** Guidelines for evaluating responses to each choice follow.

    a. Students might recognize that anxiety concerning battle can put leaders on edge and cause them to exaggerate faults and disagree about strategies.

    b. Students might respond that because of the deep and long-standing friendship between Brutus and Cassius, any disagreement upsets them greatly, and their need to reconcile is equally strong.

    c. Partial credit might be given. Students may recognize that Brutus and Cassius have different views on the future of Rome. Brutus believes in a republican government. Cassius is interested in personal power. At the moment, they are in exile, so these differences are not pressing.

    d. Students might note that Brutus and Cassius's murder of Caesar comes up in the argument and is used as the basis for suggesting that they have to rise above their petty differences. Also, their lives are at stake if they lose the battle.

Written Response

8. Responses will vary. In a model response, students should fulfill the following criteria:

- demonstrate understanding of the prompt
- clearly present a view of the ghost's dramatic function and foreshadowing (see Act II, Scene 1)
- support their ideas with at least two examples from the play. For example:
  - The ghost's appearance could be taken to

represent the venegeance that Antony has sworn he will get for Caesar.

- It can be understood as Brutus's troubled conscience rather than as a literal ghost.
- The ghost scene serves to demonstrate, as the storm in the first act does, the displeasure of the gods with the conspirators' actions.

Graphic Organizer for Active Reading, Act V

Graphic Organizer

Responses will vary. Students should quote at least one line to support their final opinions of the characters. Sample responses follow.

Antony: realistic; pragmatic; loyal (Scene 1, lines 39–44; Scene 4, lines 28–29; Scene 5, lines 68–75)

Brutus: honorable; idealistic (Scene 1, lines 110–112; Scene 5, lines 34–35)

Cassius: ambitious; cynical; loving to Brutus (Scene 1, lines 45–47, 61–62, 119–121)

Responses will vary. Sample responses follow.

1. Antony is the most admirable character because he remains loyal to Caesar and to Caesar's ideals throughout the play. He is clever, perceptive, and ambitious. He shows that he is capable of being a tyrannical ruler, but this is not inconsistent with his personality.

2. Brutus is the most villainous character because he consistently leads others to their ruin. He blunders through the play without ever realizing that people usually pursue their own interests and that life is actually unfair. Had he not been so gullible and naive, he might not have supported the murder of Caesar and convinced himself that he was performing a patriotic act.

Making Meanings, Act V

Reviewing the Text

a. The four characters are Brutus, Cassius, Antony, and Octavius.

b. In the first battle, Antony takes Cassius's army, and Brutus overthrows the troops of Octavius. After Cassius commits suicide, Antony and Octavius defeat the conspirators' remaining forces.

c. Cassius, positioned on a hill, sends Titinius to determine whether some distant troops are

Drama Study Guide: The Tragedy of Julius Caesar

118   HRW MATERIAL COPYRIGHTED UNDER NOTICE APPEARING EARLIER IN THIS WORK.

friends or enemies. He then asks Pindarus to climb higher on the hill, observe Titinius, and report what he sees. Pindarus mistakes Brutus's jubilant, victorious troops for the enemy and reports that they have captured Titinius. Cassius, believing that he sent Titinius to his doom, asks Pindarus to kill him.

d. Brutus interprets his two visions of Caesar's ghost as a sign that he must die. Now, admitting defeat in battle, he finds it more honorable to take his life than to wait for someone else to do it.

e. Antony proclaims that Brutus, alone of all the conspirators, acted from pure motives. Octavius orders that Brutus be buried with full military honors.

First Thoughts

1. Responses will vary. Some students may suggest that the deaths of Brutus and Cassius are a just punishment for the assassination of Caesar. Others may regret that much of what happened arose from misunderstanding.

Shaping Interpretations

2. Octavius emerges as the character who can and should restore order to Rome.

3. Ironies in Scene 3 include the following:
   • Cassius claims that his sight is "ever thick" (line 21), but Pindarus's clear sight does no better in revealing the truth.
   • The wreath of victory becomes a funeral wreath (lines 81–83 and 97).
   • In the end, Cassius indirectly causes Titinius's death (lines 87–90).

   Students may feel frustration at the unnecessary waste of life.

4. Both men use their last words to acknowledge that they die in retribution for Caesar's death. Cassius, however, expresses no regret for the murder, whereas Brutus again expresses sorrow, implying that he acted out of necessity rather than desire. The two scenes clearly contrast the characters of Cassius and Brutus. Cassius's speech reflects his belief in the power of revenge to motivate human action. Brutus's speech shows his belief in humankind's higher motives and his desire for Caesar to finally be at peace.

5. In Act II, Brutus spares Antony. In Act III, Brutus allows Antony to deliver a funeral oration. Brutus brings about his own downfall—not only by sparing the leader who can move and unite the people but also by giving him the opportunity to do so.

6. Responses will vary. Some students may feel that Brutus made a grave error; others may argue that his choice was right—or at least that, given Brutus's character, he could have made no other choice—while recognizing that the play's denouement supports Caesar's right to rule.

7. Caesar sets in motion all the events of the play, and he remains the acknowledged force behind all actions, even after his death. Not only do the characters continually refer to Caesar, but Shakespeare also keeps the ruler in the action— by using his corpse onstage, by introducing the ghost, and by having Cassius kill himself with the same sword that stabbed Caesar.

8. No character in *Julius Caesar* has the Aristotelian purity of a tragic hero such as Oedipus, but Brutus certainly exhibits some of the characteristics: He is noble, honorable in intent, flawed, and doomed through his own character and actions. Caesar may more nearly fit the role theoretically but not dramatically. The play does not show Caesar behaving like a tragic figure.

Extending the Text

9. *Analysis and Synthesis.* The Elizabethans did not have an automatic horror of monarchy; in their political experience a king or queen was not by definition a tyrant. Having endured violent civil wars, the English valued the peace of Elizabeth's strong reign. People today would fear both dictatorship and anarchy; some students may point out that few would envision these two "evils" as the sole options for leadership and government.

Choices: Building Your Portfolio, Act V

Critical Writing

1. As students consider how they will adapt their characters to the modern world, ask these questions:
   • How does your character feel about power?
   • How does your character feel about the people over whom he has (or wants) power?

Creative Writing

2. Before students write, plan one story or play in class together, demonstrating the essential narrative elements: setting, characters, conflict, action, climax, and resolution. Remind students to select a tone and a point of view.

ANSWER KEY

HRW MATERIAL COPYRIGHTED UNDER NOTICE APPEARING EARLIER IN THIS WORK.

119

Critical Writing

3. To begin a response to Garber's statement, have students brainstorm for a list of misunderstandings to examine. For example, you might have groups of students focus on misunderstandings that relate to one of the following:
   - Cassius
   - Caesar
   - Antony
   - Brutus

Art

4. Groups of students might prepare a "gallery walk" of their sketches. Each group should write information cards to accompany its final sketches, focusing on the overall concept (including information about the scene), scenery, props, and lighting; then, work with students to create displays.

Creative Writing

5. If Brutus were captured, his role in the conspiracy would have to be dealt with. What crime would be associated with him by his captors, and how would it affect their thinking? Also ask students how Shakespeare's various surviving characters feel at the end of the play. Have the class do some additional speculative brainstorming before students work on their new endings.

Critical Writing

6. If one of these two critical comments is used as a thesis statement, students must first summarize the statement. You might have volunteers suggest one-sentence summaries from which other students may choose.

Critical Thinking/Art

7. To facilitate this assignment, break the class into small groups and give each group a pad of self-adhesive notes. Allow each group to leaf through the play and attach notes on the pages where the group members believe transfers of power occur.

Critical Writing

8. Have the class work together to create headings under which the two political scenes might be compared. For example, two corresponding headings might be *Roman Emperor* and *U.S. President.*

Critical Writing

9. Students may find it helpful to generate questions on which to build the comparisons. This can be done in small groups or as a class. Here are a few examples:
   - What warnings about the conspiracy does Caesar have?
   - How is the relationship between Caesar and Calphurnia described?
   - How important is Decimus Brutus? Artemidorus?
   - In which account do you better understand the motives of the conspirators?

Critical Writing

10. Most choices of actors will be acceptable. As for choice of setting, make sure that it is relevant to the play in some way. You might have students pick a single scene and stage it in more detail or have them cover the whole play in a general manner. Have them consider such elements as costumes, sound effects and props. Artistic students might want to sketch the set or make a model of it.

Research

11. Encourage students to use a variety of reference sources and tools, from history textbooks to electronic databases. Be sure they consult at least one primary source as well as secondary ones. For this assignment you might have students work together in small groups.

Critical Writing

12. Students' responses will vary but should demonstrate a thorough understanding of the event. Responses should include a thesis statement and elaboration in the form of supporting details, examples, and illustrations.

Language Link Mini-Lesson, Act V

Try It Out

Evaluate students' speeches not just on word-for-word accuracy but also on interpretation. You or your students might use the following statements to rate each reading from 1 (poor) to 5 (exceptional).

1 Quotes the speech correctly.

2 Presents the speech in a natural, conversational manner.

3 Uses pitch and volume well.

Drama Study Guide: The Tragedy of Julius Caesar

4 Uses a good rate of speech with appropriate pauses.

5 Captures the essential meaning of the speech.

In the next few weeks, invite students to report to the class on any occasion when they use or refer to one of these speeches in conversation.

Words to Own Worksheet, Act V

Developing Vocabulary

Sentences will vary. Sample responses follow. Vocabulary words are shown in italics.

1. Warring factions can sometimes reach an accord through a serious *parley*.

2. *Vile* behavior will not be tolerated in the minimum-security prison.

3. A *cur* would not make a successful nursing-home assistant.

4. Roman generals relied on competent *legions*.

5. Dejected and *disconsolate*, Samuel retreated to his room to lick the wounds of heartbreak.

6. "If you have *misconstrued* my efforts, please be assured I want only what's best for the company," the manager told her employees.

7. The hyena's *entrails* were food for vultures after the lion had disemboweled it.

8. "No *tarrying*, children; pick up your belongings, and let's go," said the mother.

9. Human *bondage* is despicable to human rights activists, as well as to other groups.

10. I am honored that you will *bestow* your presence upon me.

Language Link Worksheet, Act V

Responses will vary. Sample responses follow.

Exercise A

1. Tone, volume, or rate of speech should be changed for emphasis.

2. It is a parenthetical phrase, to be delivered with a pause and lower volume.

3. a short pause

4. *these*

5. There is no pause at the end of the line.

6. with a pause and in a lower volume

7. Because it is repeated, it is underlined so it will be given special emphasis.

8. No pause is planned.

Exercise B

This was the noblest Roman of them all. //

All the conspirators, / save only he /

Did that they did in envy of great Caesar; //

He, only in a general honest thought

And common good to all, / made one of them.

His life was gentle, / and the elements

So mixed in him that Nature might stand up

And say to all the world, / "This was a man!" //

Literary Elements Worksheet, Act V

Understanding the Tragic Hero

Responses will vary. Sample responses follow.

Characteristic—is the main character. *Julius Caesar*—All events are related to the assassination. *Brutus*—There would be no assassination without him.

Characteristic—shows evidence of high rank. *Julius Caesar*—rules Rome. *Brutus*—called a noble Roman by all.

Characteristic—shows nobility of character. *Julius Caesar*—remembers the people in his will. *Brutus*—allows Antony to live and to speak.

Characteristic—is marred by tragic flaw or fatal mistake in judgment. *Julius Caesar*—too proud to take advice to stay home. *Brutus*—lets others convince him of the need to kill Caesar.

Characteristic—gains self-knowledge and wisdom. *Julius Caesar*—not applicable. *Brutus*—repents of killing Caesar.

Characteristic—comes to an unhappy end. *Julius Caesar*—is killed. *Brutus*—commits suicide.

Applying Skills

Responses will vary.

Reader's Response

Responses will vary.

Test, Act V

Thoughtful Reading

1. a   **2.** c   **3.** d   **4.** c   **5.** b

Expanded Response

6. Responses will vary. Students should use at least one example from the play to support their ideas. The best answers are **a** and **b.** Guidelines for evaluating responses to each choice follow.

    a. Students might recognize that the deaths of Cassius and Brutus avenge Caesar's death and that both characters allude to Caesar just before dying.

    b. Students might recognize that there is a sense that order has been or soon will be restored, and the injustice of removing Caesar has been put right.

    c. Partial credit might be given. Students might note that Antony acknowledges that Brutus was truly motivated by honorable impulses, even if Cassius and the other conspirators were not. Also, it is Brutus's concept of honor that leads him to choose suicide rather than be captured.

7. Responses will vary. Sample responses follow.

Brutus. Tragic—He is concerned with the good of Rome, not with personal gain. He is honest and trusts others. *Not Tragic*—He takes part in a violent murder on the basis of potential tyranny on Caesar's part.

Caesar. Tragic—He is a military hero and is popular with the people and capable of maintaining a strong, unified Rome. *Not Tragic*—He is vain, arrogant, ambitious, and blind to flattery.

Written Response

8. Responses will vary. In a model response, students should fulfill the following criteria:
* demonstrate understanding of the prompt
* clearly describe at least two contradictory feelings or actions in the last act
* support their ideas with at least two examples from Act V. For example:
  * Antony calls Brutus the noblest Roman although he had taunted him earlier for leading them to war.
  * Brutus takes his own life even though he had said earlier he disapproved of his father-in-law's suicide.
  * Octavius speaks of the "glories" of the day, although what we have just seen is a great deal of violence and death.

* The image of eagles and vultures in Cassius's omens is a contradiction reflected in the roles of Antony and Octavius: Both men are eagles (victors), but they achieve victory, like vultures, only through death (the deaths of Cassius and Brutus).

Test, the Play as a Whole

Responding to Literature

Responses will vary. Sample responses follow.

1. *Character:* Caesar. *Choice:* He ignores the warnings from the soothsayer and his wife about entering the Senate. *Reason:* He argues that he as a leader must not show fear and that death comes to all, so why fear it? *Consequence:* He is assassinated.

2. *Character:* Brutus. *Philosophy:* He is a Stoic, one who values self-control. *Action:* Because of this he does not show his feelings outwardly when told of Portia's death.

3. Responses will vary. In a model response, students should fulfill the following criteria:
* demonstrate understanding of the prompt
* clearly describe how Shakespeare suggests the setting through language and action
* support their ideas with examples from one scene in the play. For example: the scene in which the conspirators meet in the street, talking vividly of the way nature is in turmoil and huddling together as if frightened though pretending not to be.

4. Responses will vary. In a model response, students should fulfill the following criteria:
* demonstrate understanding of the prompt
* clearly describe the way in which one particular passion is dramatized in the play
* support their ideas with a discussion of two scenes from the play. For example:
  * the violent murder in the Senate
  * the discovery of Cassius's body by Brutus
  * Octavius's victory at the end of the play

Paraphrasing

Responses may vary. Sample responses follow.

5. Cowards suffer the fear of death throughout their lives; the valiant experience death only once.

6. For Brutus, as you know, was Caesar's favorite.

Drama Study Guide: The Tragedy of Julius Caesar

7. After people die, their evil deeds are remembered; their good ones are often buried with them (that is, they are forgotten).

Testing the Genre

Understanding Vocabulary

1. c   **2.** b   **3.** a   **4.** b   **5.** b

Thoughtful Reading

6. d   **7.** b   **8.** c   **9.** d   **10.** b

Expanded Response

11. Responses will vary. Students should use at least one example from the excerpt to support their ideas. The best answers are **b** and **d**. Guidelines for evaluating responses to each choice follow.

   a. Partial credit might be given. Lady Macbeth never loses her resolve to kill Duncan as Macbeth temporarily does, yet she will not do the actual stabbing herself.

   b. Students may say that Lady Macbeth's determination to see that Macbeth keeps their bloody bargain is fierce, especially as expressed in her image of dashing out the brains of a child.

   c. Partial credit might be given. Lady Macbeth keeps her word, but what she resolves to do is hardly honorable.

   d. Students might point out that Lady Macbeth's implacable ambition to see Macbeth king and herself queen drives her to urge— even insist—that Macbeth murder Duncan.

Written Response

12. Responses will vary. In a model response, students should fulfill the following criteria:
   • demonstrate understanding of the prompt
   • clearly compare and contrast Brutus and Macbeth, specifically exploring their motives for murder and their misgivings
   • support their ideas with at least two examples from both *The Tragedy of Julius Caesar* and the excerpt from *The Tragedy of Macbeth.* For example:
     • Both men allow others to persuade them to commit certain acts (Brutus allows Cassius; Macbeth allows Lady Macbeth).
     • Both profess to love the rulers they slay.
     • Brutus wants to kill Caesar out of fear that Caesar will become a dictator and all Romans will lose their freedom. Macbeth, however, only wants power for himself and his family.
     • Brutus meets with tragedy because of his inability to recognize the baser motives of others; Macbeth meets his tragic end because he doesn't have the strength to resist his own baser motives and the single-minded ambition of his wife.